SAVAGE GODS, SILVER GHOSTS

SAVAGE GODS,

in the wild with TED HUGHES

SILVER GHOSTS

EHOR BOYANOWSKY

DOUGLAS & MCINTYRE
Vancouver / Toronto / Berkeley

Douglas & McIntyre
A division of D&M Publishers Inc.
2323 Quebec Street, Suite 201
Vancouver BC Canada V5T 4S7
www.douglas-mcintyre.com

Library and Archives Canada Cataloguing in Publication
Boyanowsky, Ehor, 1943–
Savage gods, silver ghosts : in the wild with Ted Hughes / Ehor Boyanowsky.
Includes bibliographical references.

ISBN 978-1-55365-323-3

1. Hughes, Ted, 1930–1998. 2. Boyanowsky, Ehor, 1943– ——Friends and associates.
3. Fishing—British Columbia. 4. Poets, English—20th century—Biography.
5. Psychologists—Canada—Biography. 1. Title.

PR6058.U37Z675 2009   821'.914   C2009-903368-2

Editing by John Burns
Jacket design by Peter Cocking and Naomi MacDougall
Text design by Naomi MacDougall
Jacket photograph of Ted Hughes fishing on the Dean River
in 1987 copyright © 2009 by Ehor Boyanowsky
Printed and bound in Canada by Friesens
Printed on acid-free paper that is forest friendly (100% post-consumer
recycled paper) and has been processed chlorine free.
Distributed in the U.S. by Publishers Group West

Original material for this book comes largely from the journals
of the author, conversations with other individuals present at various meetings,
correspondence between Ted Hughes and the author, notes taken from the
Totem Flyfishers Dean River Logbook and some recorded material.

This book is based on the personal recollections of the author and
does not represent an authorized record of the words of Ted Hughes.

Douglas & McIntyre gratefully acknowledges the financial support of the
Canada Council for the Arts, the British Columbia Arts Council, the
Province of British Columbia through the Book Publishing Tax Credit
and the Government of Canada through the Book Publishing Industry
Development Program (BPIDP) for our publishing activities.

For Lesia and Steve,
who were always there for me

In memoriam:
Nick Hughes, 1962–2009

CONTENTS

PROLOGUE *1*

1 / Inventing the Poet *7*

2 / Tales of Dean River Steelhead *22*

3 / Art on the Thompson *50*

4 / Halcyon Days *67*

5 / A House Divided *98*

6 / Re-creation in Ancient Celtic Lands *130*

7 / A Season of Celebrations *158*

8 / Death and Renewal *179*

ACKNOWLEDGEMENTS *197*

BRITISH
COLUMBIA

Map B

Map A

U.S.A.

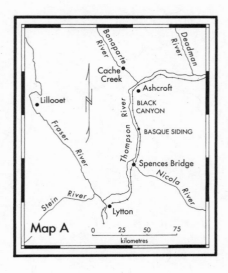

Bonaparte River

Deadman River

Cache Creek

Ashcroft

Lillooet

BLACK CANYON

Thompson River

BASQUE SIDING

Fraser River

Spences Bridge

Nicola River

Stein River

Lytton

Map A

0   25   50   75

kilometres

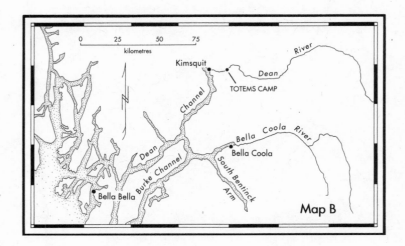

0   25   50   75

kilometres

Kimsquit

Dean River

TOTEMS CAMP

Channel

Bella Coola River

Dean

Bella Coola

Burke Channel

South Bentinck Arm

Bella Bella

Map B

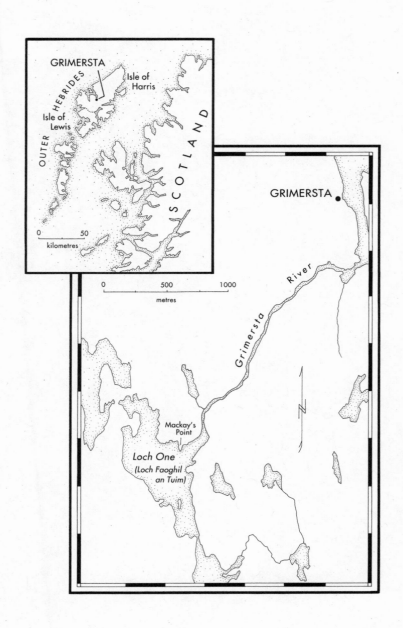

PROLOGUE

Flashes of light—a fusillade from the ambush of paparazzi—punctuate the gloom of a London May morning. Three of us move through the onlookers to the great doors of Westminster Abbey. Stewards lead the way past soaring gothic columns resounding with the sonorous waves of a Bach fugue. We take our seats in Poets' Corner under a dark bust of William Blake as the intonations of the Westminster Choir rise above the dying echoes of the great organ. A hand on my sleeve. "Dad, I don't feel too well." I glance at Alexei, my twelve-year-old. His first time in a great mediaeval church, he is nearly overcome. "It's like heaven," he whispers. We rise as the queen mother, as lovely and fragile as an autumn leaf, enters upon the arm of her grandson, the Prince of Wales.

More than seventeen hundred of us gather in the church this afternoon in 1999. That number includes members of the royal family, politicians and conservationists, academics, anglers, socialites and many poets, among them Nobel Laureate Seamus Heaney and Andrew Motion, soon to be named Poet Laureate. Finally, a procession of clerics, including the controversial dean of Westminster, Wesley Carr. Most are here as admirers of an extraordinary man, thinker and poet, Ted Hughes. It is an occasion created by his wife, Carol, to give thanks for the life and work of the Poet Laureate who died in October at the age of sixty-eight.

There is much music, from the lyricism of thirteenth-century Scots balladeer Thomas the Rhymer adapted by Ted for his friend, Iranian folksinger Shusha Guppy, who accompanies herself on guitar ("When you are old enough to love you will be taken prisoner by the blossom of apple and pear . . .") to, at the close, the haunting melody of *Spem in alium* by sixteenth-century English composer Thomas Tallis and sung by the Tallis Scholars. I think back to my first visit to Devon when I commented to Ted on the beauty of the countryside, the air rich with history and thick with ghosts, and he retorted with delight: "Yes, and can you see why I love British Columbia where the air is light and unencumbered? I feel freed when I'm there."

We met through a common acquaintance, a journalist who wrote for *The Times* of London. Ted's first visit in 1986 to read at the University of British Columbia turned into annual two-week sojourns spent usually on the Dean River, more than 450 kilometres northwest of Vancouver, occasionally in Devon and Scotland as well. It was around our campfire on the Dean, on a September night with a barrage of northern lights rippling and crackling overhead, that he told me how coming to British Columbia had rekindled a part of him long dormant.

For Ted, British Columbia was the road not taken. As a boy in the Yorkshire Pennines he would tag along with his older brother, Gerald, on hunting, fishing and trapping excursions. "He was my retriever," Gerald tells me in the foyer of the Abbey. Around campfires on the moor, Gerald and Ted would discuss the wonders they found in the books of Roderick Haig-Brown, a British expatriate who settled in Campbell River on Vancouver Island and enthralled young people the world over with his stories of fishing, hunting and life in the woods. They made a pact to emigrate together to British Columbia, but Gerald moved to Australia and Ted went to Cambridge, then no farther than Devon. In spirit and gesture, he once told me, I reminded him of his brother: "But that doesn't do much for you?" So moved was I to hear that characterization, I fear now that perhaps I didn't convey enough of the pleasure I took from his company.

In the Abbey, speakers read extensively from Ted's works. The poems range from nightmarish memories of the First World War that, left unspoken, haunted his father, to "Anniversary," wherein he evoked the death of his mother "in her feathers of flame," and "That Morning," in which he contrasted watching salmon in a stream with boyhood memories of endless flights of bombers in the night sky.

Ted's words fill the Abbey, igniting memories. Among those memories is that hushed recital hall at the University of British Columbia, where Ted crafted a setting for each poem so revealing that it made perfectly transparent images that the ordinary reader often finds at once complex and obscure. The joy and wonder that glowed in his handsome, craggy face when he beheld his first ghostlike steelhead on the Dean. The day we wrote a poem together to celebrate the sixtieth anniversary of my wife's grandparents—four iterations in two hours—while packing to fly out to fish next morning.

When the rivers and wild salmon of Britain and British Columbia came under threat of extinction, Ted was there, no longer reluctant to speak out or write essays, though he was a shy and reserved man, loath to be in the public eye—perhaps because once that reserve was breached, his inclination was to give of himself entirely. When my personal world darkened, he would phone every week and write me long letters generously offering his own life experiences to provide meaning and even optimism for the future.

Ted's life had its own dark chapters, as his friend and collaborator Seamus Heaney alludes to standing before us in the Abbey: "Ted was a great man and a great poet through his wholeness, simplicity and unfaltering truth to his sense of the world. That sense of the world was epic and stern, in that it constantly beheld behind the business of the usual, a sacred drama being enacted."

I'm struck by how much Heaney's words reflect a poem I'm sure he never read. Ted wrote "The Bear" as part of a logbook entry on the Dean and offered it to us to use as we wished. Describing a storm it recalls:

5

> The thousand-mile humping of mountains
> That looked immovable, was in a frenzy,
> Metabolism of stars, melt of snows—
> Was shivering to its ecstasy in the Steelhead.
> This actually was the love-act that had brought them
> Out of everywhere, squirming and leaping,
> And that had brought us too—besotted voyeurs—
> Trying to hook ourselves into it.

I can still clearly recall his voice as he lay by the campfire on the Thompson River pointing out the Perseids meteor showers to a very young Alexei, regaling us all with ghost stories, his spirit spilling over with the joy of rediscovering the universe through the eyes of a child. On my granddaughter's first birthday Ted penned a verse that we stuck on a rocket and fired off over Howe Sound. At his urging— to assure good fortune, he said—no copy was kept.

Later, we discussed what we would do differently if we had our lives to begin again. I presumed, given his great achievements, that Ted would not change his career. Not so. "I might want to come back as a Sufi." One who meditates on the secrets of the universe, pursuing inner truth and peace and imparting those insights to the people in stories? A light year away from the public glare of Poet Laureate.

Heaney goes on to place Ted in the pantheon of great poets from Cædmon to Shakespeare to Hopkins. There is silence. Then a powerful Yorkshire voice fills the sacred space: "Fear no more the heat of the sun." It is Ted reading from Shakespeare's *Cymbeline,* ending with "Golden Lads, and Girls all must, / As chimney-Sweepers come to dust." The disembodied recording brings home the realization that my friend is dead.

6

1 / INVENTING THE POET

I have been to many poetry readings. They are usually held in cobweb-ridden bookstores or classrooms with the ambience of broom closets. And they are never standing room only. When my wife, Vicky, and I, with one-month-old Alexei in tow, arrive at the University of British Columbia Recital Hall, hundreds of people are already seated. It is August 19, 1986. Dozens, many with granny glasses and knitted toques adorning their ratty coiffures, are milling about in a quandary outside. Not having expected such a grand venue to sell out weeks in advance, they are left to wait in the foyer for the reception. Some appear heartbroken, some angry, others merely dazed or, more likely, stoned. We sit towards the back as a hush falls. The Victoria writer David Day, fresh scrubbed and boyish,

is on the podium describing his meeting and acquaintanceship with Hughes. (He briefly dated Frieda, Hughes's daughter.) This is a giant space made for orchestras and great
choirs. How will one voice merely reading poetry be able to
command its attention?

8   Then a veritable giant, moving with geological force like
a hulking mass of the cliffs of Dover broken off and dressed
in tweedy brown, mounts the podium. As he starts to speak,
in a gentle rumble, a silence falls upon the room. He introduces each poem with an elucidation of his circumstances in
writing it. Hughes describes coming to Cambridge to read
English and how, one night, struggling with a literary cri-
tique, he dreamed of a fox with a bloody severed head, standing at the foot of his bed. "You're killing me," it tells him.
Hughes interprets the dream to mean that his psyche has
warned him that, should he continue to study English literature, his creative energies will be quickly spent. Soon after,
Hughes transferred to anthropology. He describes the importance of animal imagery and how writing poems is like hunting animals, as he did as a boy with his gamekeeper brother,
Gerald, his idol and mentor in all things wild. Then he reads
from "The Thought-Fox":

> It enters the dark hole of the head.
> The window is starless still; the clock ticks,
> The page is printed.

I understand now how women, and men too, fall in love with Hughes, shy as he is, for once he gives of himself, he holds nothing back. The listener is thrilled to be privy to the creative process.

Hughes describes how, while living in the centre of the city and caring for his fretful infant daughter, he listened to the wolves caged in the London Zoo, her crying bringing them running. I grew up in the boreal forest of Northern Ontario but never knew more about wolves than pelts brought in to the Hudson's Bay Company store by bounty hunters, white and aboriginal. Soon after that reading, though, Vicky and I helicopter into the Sustut River in north-central British Columbia and, on the first day, she calls out to me. A magnificent black male wolf is eyeing her from the beach as she wades the river, casting her fly for steelhead. That night a chorus of spine-tingling howlers serenades the full moon.

Too soon the reading is over and the deluge of listeners pours from the hall enrapt over what they have heard. Then, Ted Hughes. "Ehor, good to meet you. Can you wait until I talk to those who are waiting? Then let's go eat. I thought I was going to be fed and have been subsisting on a liquid diet—I'll tell you later."

I stand watching Ted listen intently to each person in line, answering every question after pausing for reflection, stuffing into his bulging pockets sheaves of poems thrust upon him by earnest earth-toned poets, weaving from a surfeit of alcohol (his companions beforehand having somewhat mischievously taken him on a tour of the strip bars Vancouver is known for) and a lack of sustenance (in the U.K. the hosts normally provide dinner first). His hair is lank with grease, his face a panoply of sweat, his body sways as he sips yet more wine, but his eyes are unblinking and alert.

Finally the last in the long lineup floats past us. "My God, what a man, what a kind person. Way better than I ever expected. I can't believe it!" He disappears in the direction of his little cadre of macramé-loving acolytes.

"Let's get out of here," Ted mutters. "I am about to faint."

Minutes later we are sitting in a late-night Greek restaurant on Fourth Avenue. The wine is flowing and, after a feeding frenzy during which little can be heard above the crunching of bone and the sucking of marrow, a four-way conversation ensues. Linda Rogers, an attractive, bright poet and writer, is besieging Ted with questions and witty comments. Ignoring her, Ted is bombarding me with questions about fishing, which I am trying to deflect and transform into a general discussion. Vicky is eyeing Alexei worriedly, given it is nearly one in the morning. He, however, is dead to the world despite the chatter and music. I feel a rush of pleasure: the world is unfolding as I had hoped.

. . .

I FIRST ENCOUNTERED the poetry of Ted Hughes a quarter century before. I was sitting in the dingy office of *Folio* magazine at the University of Western Ontario, pondering

a sexually explicit memoir by an undergraduate that may
have been the best-written story I had received but that
had already triggered controversy: the faculty adviser had
resigned; the printer, who also did a United Church magazine, insisted on handling it personally. It was 1963 and the
social revolution had begun.

Jerry Rogers walked in. Despite his apple pie demeanour,
Jerry was the most self-consciously literary person I knew at
UWO, equal parts Norman Mailer, Allen Ginsberg and Jack
Kerouac. In first year we would stay up all night drinking
and reading and reciting poetry, until at some point, fuelled
by booze, Rogers would challenge me to a fight. That was
usually no problem. He weighed about a hundred and sixty
pounds. I was six foot three and a tight end on the junior var-
sity football team.

"Here," he said, tossing me a thin volume. "Here's
something a boy from Northern Ontario can appreciate." I
expected a collection of Robert Service. Not exactly. It was
Lupercal by Ted Hughes, a poet I had never heard of. I leafed
through. And then I read "Hawk Roosting" and its preda-
tors that "in sleep rehearse perfect kills and eat." I was trans-
fixed. There was an immediacy to Hughes's poetry that
rivalled the experience of actual wilderness, of animals going
about making a living, and that, but for the grace of God,
you might be part of—as prey. I have sought that unfiltered
experience my whole life—where you tread unprotected,
should you dare.

I was thrilled to discover that Ted Hughes's first volume of poetry, *The Hawk in the Rain*, published eight years before, had received a prize adjudicated by a panel that included no less than W.H. Auden, Robert Lowell and Stephen Spender. My own interests, which ranged from the northern bush to the vagaries of human love and hate, seemed somehow vindicated in the face of the overburden of urban torpor dominating contemporary poetry.

Some fifteen years later, I was at Simon Fraser University in criminology and planning to take a sabbatical from my work as a criminal psychologist. I was invited by the London School of Economics to spend time there lecturing to graduate students, and so, having for many years dabbled in nonacademic writing and being in the process of reinventing myself, I felt the time was ripe to test the waters. I sent off a batch of poems and stories of fishing to Nick Lyons, a New York City English professor and publisher whose column for *Fly Fisherman* magazine I very much admired. I had been told by a friend of his whom I met on a salmon trip to Newfoundland that he was a kind man and very supportive of young writers. Lyons wrote back encouraging me and asked if I was familiar with Ted Hughes, whom he described as an English poet who had married the American Sylvia Plath but was, in his opinion, the better poet. With the letter he included Hughes's "October Salmon."

Through a decade and a half of marriage, becoming a father, getting a PhD, becoming a professor and a father once again, I had almost lost touch with the power and sustaining beauty of Hughes's work. But now, I read of the spawned-out salmon dressed by Death "in her clownish regimental, her badges and decorations." In a time of deep depression from a failed marriage, when I was desperately trying to save myself by jump-starting afresh in England's old and venerable culture, I found myself imbued with the excitement of Hughes's writing once again.

I launched into a whirlwind trip lecturing in London, Cambridge, Oxford and Scotland in the parallel universes of criminal psychology and wilderness photography. One night, I mentioned my interest in Hughes's work to my host, who let slip that the co-author of his most recent book on fishing actually knew Hughes, having taken a poetry workshop in one of his residences.

I decided to send Hughes a cycle of poems about the seasons of the steelhead, the mystical fighting salmon of British Columbia:

The rains of November have come and gone
The river swelled and surged and subsided.
We rose in the dark, stoked with coffee and eggs
    and rashers of bacon
To head up past the gate into the lost world of
    the watershed . . .
Silence but for the soft murmur of our boots in
    the downy snow
And the rhythmic panting of the setters
    forging ahead . . .

For a long time I heard nothing, which I attributed either to the fact Hughes did not want to humiliate me or to the fact that he had recently been named Poet Laureate by Queen Elizabeth (select company that includes Edmund Spenser, Ben Jonson, John Dryden, William Wordsworth and Alfred Lord Tennyson).

14

Then, after returning to Vancouver and meeting the woman I hoped would become the love of my life and, after almost two years of romantic and domestic bliss, discovering she was pregnant, eloping to Carcross in Yukon for a spontaneous Klondike wedding and finally becoming a father for the third time, I got an odd-looking letter written on Alaska Cooperative Fishery Research Unit stationery. Odd, for it appeared not to be an official missive, despite its academic masthead. For a moment I assumed it was from some biologist interested in B.C. steelhead stocks or fishing generally, as the salutation was a very impersonal "Dear Ehor Boyanowsky." I began to read it rather cursorily as I listened to the CBC six o'clock news. The handwriting, however, was definitely European, with idiosyncratic swirls that started off very legible but as the writer got wound up with enthusiasm, a condition I could relate to, became increasingly compressed and hieroglyphical.

As I struggled through the script, a spark of recognition ignited inside my brain and I believe my hand trembled as I turned off the radio, so I had to start again from the beginning, this time savouring the dense text. It was from Hughes, sitting in a cabin in the Alaska bush while visiting his son, Nicholas, a graduate student at University of Alaska Fairbanks. And this was no polite, perfunctory reply to my letter and package of writing.

He spoke of how he had put off responding to my letter until he had the time to do it justice, since most of the correspondence he had to attend to now as laureate was not of his choosing. That though he was in Alaska, far removed from my poems and photos, they were nevertheless very much to his taste and that gauging from what I had sent him, he was in all probability one of my keenest fans. That he was going to be presenting in Victoria and then Vancouver and, if I were interested, he would love to get together. He went on to describe how he had been visiting his son, a fisheries biologist, for the past several years but had messed up the timing this year so was reduced to sitting in the cabin writing or serving as his son's research assistant. Most poignantly, his interest in British Columbia had been piqued by a fellow he had met in Scotland who had been fishing steelhead on one of our northern rivers and had been battered black and blue, terrorized by their power. He had shown Hughes a book, John Fennelly's *Steelhead Paradise*, that had set his heart pounding. He ended by lamenting how a court case in New York—which I later found out had been mounted by the psychiatrist of his late wife, Sylvia Plath, who felt she had been mischaracterized as a lesbian in Plath's prize-winning novel, *The Bell Jar*—had ensnared him merely for being the executor of Plath's estate. But most important, he wanted to make arrangements to visit British Columbia in the future.

Hughes had read my letter; in fact, had read my poems. And although circumspect and respectful of any special knowledge I might have—careful, even, not to seem too intrusive—he seemed to want, I felt, reading between the lines, to establish a beachhead and find out about steelhead. It appeared he wanted us to fish together. And against all odds there was a lovely gentleness about him, about his attitude towards his visit with his son—a refreshing contrast to his public image created by vilification at the hands of self-important mindless radical groups at both ends of the political spectrum: hatred-fuelled self-righteousness that my experience in the New Left of the 1960s and my extensive research into group pressure processes, conformity and gangs had made me intimately familiar with. In fact, at first bluff, Hughes appeared to be the sort of man I could spend a lot of time with, both on the river and off. I recalled how, upon visiting several times with Ann Haig-Brown, she had lamented the fact I had been too shy to contact her late husband, Roderick, the only other writer I had ever cared to meet. Perhaps, despite the risk involved, contacting the person whose work I admired might sometimes not puncture my admiration but could be immensely gratifying. It would turn out I had no idea.

. . .

FOR THE UNINITIATED, the passion (even obsession) for fishing Atlantic salmon and its mystical West Coast cousin, the steelhead, is bemusing at best, worthy of disdain at worst.

It is no exaggeration to claim that careers have been compromised, marriages have foundered and fortunes lost in its pursuit. In one of the most elegant and amusing essays on the phenomenon, David Goodman, president of Red Capital, a Washington, D.C., merchant bank, who claims to fish for up to two hundred days a year, describes the rapid demise of his marriage: "As our protracted Norwegian fishing was about to end," he writes in *Wild Steelhead and Salmon* magazine, "a rare offer came to fish the Alta. When I invited my bride, she imploded in tears, which my fishing companion, Bo Ivanovic, a more seasoned salmonist and husband, interpreted as 'probably not an unqualified endorsement.'" The marriage lasted a year.

Over that first late-night dinner, through dolmades and retsina, Ted is charming, almost childlike, in his desire to milk me for as much info as he can about steelhead, "that most glamorous of fish." I recognize the condition, the almost palpable desire he is experiencing. He has read John Goddard's article in *Salmon and Trout* magazine on an expedition to the Dean, the world's greatest steelhead river, that John took with me and my friend Jay Rowland of the Totem Flyfishers, and he is beside himself with excitement. I tell him how the Dean flows out of Tweedsmuir Park in the Chilcotin, a perfect alchemy of headwater, meandering chalk stream transmogrifying into a broad, tumbling coastal river as it pierces the stronghold of the Coast Mountain Range to enter the Pacific Ocean north of Bella Coola.

I describe its aquamarine water, its giant bluffs, the remnant ice patch looming over our camp on the river. Downstream, a string of snow-capped mountains; upstream, the horizon a sleeping woman. The forest, being farther north and stripped of its old-growth trees in the past three decades, is not as lush as other coastal regions, but the hills have "greened up" nicely and the cottonwoods along the shifting and crumbling banks of the flood plain provide a stately row of sheltering, nurturing sentinels for the river. The conditions created are somehow ideal for the river to become a fecund nursery to a race of some of the largest, most powerful steelhead in the world. A race that returns to its natal stream from June to October, snarling and snapping at proffered flies: silver ghosts making their way to the spawning grounds of the following spring. Because they shall not spawn for months they have unprecedented resources of muscle and flesh. The hooked fish surge, tumbling downstream, sometimes totally uncontrollable, as the angler stumbles after on giant cobbles, the worries of a sordid life forgotten. It is an addiction.

When the Dean River was discovered by outsiders in the early 1960s, it was only for the very wealthy—who came in to fish with expert guides—or loggers and their executive bosses who took time off from denuding the valley to kill as many steelhead as they could. Then the B.C. angler and the "American steelhead bum" (a romanticized vagabond akin to the surfer or skier who travels the world seeking the perfect wave or mountain) discovered a paradise of which they had only dreamed. Some set up camp for the summer. For many years, the Totem Flyfishers, thanks to the selfless efforts of former president Bob Taylor and a few cohorts, have mounted camp expeditions for members and guests over a period of five or six weeks from late July to September.

It can be a wilderness idyll or a nightmare fraught with anxiety and peril. Airplanes have crashed on the stony strip at Kimsquit, the site of the vacated aboriginal camp at the mouth of the Dean. For years, Felix Lederer, a jolly recluse who claimed to have won his wife, Ella, in a poker game, usually ran the group and its equipment up the logging road in a gasping green pickup. On our first trip the truck had broken an axle, and so, in the midst of a blazing heat wave, we had to hump the essentials up the canyon on our backs. On several occasions, floods from monsoon rains washed out most of the week; on others, grizzlies ripped up the rubber inflatable boats we used to cross the river. On one trip a recalcitrant black bear lay in wait for us to lower our food packsack, then raced us to it when it hit the ground. Sometimes competing steelheaders would rise earlier and earlier to be the first into the pool: the ultimate was Bob York, who packed a raft up the logging road in the middle of the night to get to a pool before dawn. Sometimes the fish would be virtually wiped out at sea by the rapacious gillnet fleet and never show up, making the week's sojourn futile. Other times the heat in the blast furnace of the valley would be Sahara-like, melting the glaciers and turning the river the colour and texture of mercury.

Ted is enthralled. His eyes light up when I suggest that perhaps something could be arranged. "Just tell me when and where," he blurts out. Upon handshakes and hugs all around, we bid each other goodbye, promising to write as we part at two that summer night. Vicky and I cruise home in dreamlike serenity to Deep Cove, a village nestled on the slopes of the fiord known as Indian Arm. What originally attracted me to it, along with its proximity to the campus where I teach, was that it had been the Vancouver area residence of the British expatriate Malcolm Lowry, one of my favourite writers. Lowry had lived in a shack in nearby Dollarton while writing—actually dictating to his wife, since he suffered from physical writer's block—*Under the Volcano*, one of the great novels of the twentieth century. I was amazed by the fact that Lowry not only rewrote *Under the Volcano* several times—at least once completely as the manuscript was lost in a fire in the shack—but found time each day, summer and winter, to swim across the inlet to the pub I knew as the Admiral, a strip bar where friends and I would sometimes stop for a drink on the way home (purely out of respect for the writer, of course). In the 1990s a smaller section of the bar was briefly turned into the Malcolm Lowry Pub, which hosted poetry and prose readings and alternative bands. It was a wonderful era.

Looking for the location of that long-gone shack among the giant trees of Dollarton Park comprised one of the few pilgrimages I ever undertook. I would often take my dogs, and occasionally my younger daughter, Thea, to the beaches there to wade and cast a fly for foraging cutthroat trout. Bemused passersby, when told I was fishing for trout with my wandlike rod in the massive waters of Burrard Inlet, would nod their heads sympathetically and move on.

2 / TALES OF DEAN RIVER STEELHEAD

The Dean in late August is low and cool and clear, but dark—almost sinister in the grey overcast. We find the inflatable boat battened down against sudden winds on a gravel beach along the river downstream. Dragging it to the water, we row over to the wooded left bank of the Victoria Run, a frothing throat becoming a deep boulder-strewn belly with a lovely fanlike tail that holds its depth at three to four feet and so makes ideal water for the steelhead, that seagoing rainbow trout now categorized as a Pacific salmon, to track, follow and engulf a fly. Its willingness to rise to the dry fly, even in the frigid temperatures of a December river's water, makes the steelhead, mythic in its power and magnitude, especially prized.

The river hisses against the oars and lashes at the inflatable raft, trying to force our craft downstream through the rapids into a looming logjam. Hunkered down on the pontoon, Ted looks around, feeling the river's power; he drinks in the spicy aroma of the great cedars, and his face is wet from the spray, his gaze filled with the sweep of muscular granite cliffs shouldering the banks and the undulating horizon of glacier-topped peaks upstream and down.

There is always a discomfiting suspension of the familiar, of the normal reassurances of civilization, in true wilderness, in the domain of the savage gods. For all to go well on a remote river—in fact, merely to survive—you rely entirely on whatever skills and resources you can marshal. Layers of dull, insulating habit peel off, and the senses, the very nerve endings, go into overdrive. It is a reawakening that the bush dweller experiences every day but the urbanite pays for dearly (the intensity can startle and the fear and dread overwhelm). You are less than insignificant, it suggests, no more than a mud wasp. The feeling of relief is humbling and reassuring. Time to fish.

The victory cries of our camp mates, Jay Rowland and Ron Cordes, hooking into steelhead ululate in our ears as Ted and I trundle downstream over the cobbles. Should we have stayed with them rather than gambling on the glories of the left bank of what's become the most productive pool on the Dean River?

Ambivalence about which pool to fish at any given

moment is endemic to steelhead fishing. One holding water may be tauntingly empty, whereas another just passed over may produce strike after strike. The main pool at the foot of the cutbank upon which we are encamped we call the Home Pool. Others call it the Totem Pool, for we have camped there for several years. It is a wonder of holding water, with its head formed by the spilling of a wide lip of the Cottonwood Pool just above that is ideal for fishing the dry fly. The Cottonwood is a fine piece of flywater comprising, in its best part, a smooth shallow glide fringed on the far side with great creaking deciduous trees but rather short in length, perhaps only fifty yards.

The Home Pool, however, is in a class by itself. It runs from the head where the Cottonwood empties, through a rather narrow throat ridden with boulders where steelhead may lie but best fished with a dry fly because of the swiftness of the current, to the big, easy belly bounded on the camp side by a logjam featuring most prominently a long fallen tree jutting out into the pool. When the water is high the log undulates in the current, becoming an obstacle deadly to river navigation. But if the pool is fished from the far side by casting across and just above it, that section is ideal for a deep-sunk fly, for when the fish are in they pile up like cordwood in that belly, strafing any deep-sunk fly swinging by. It is where bonanzas of ten fish hooked often occur. I like it best just below where the pool fans out into a tail that can be plied with a dry fly from both sides, and I have stood there

knee-deep in the current, raising fish after fish, swirling after
and whacking my fly in playful malevolence. After awhile
you become so rattled it is difficult to hold the rod still as
the river swells and rises announcing the attack of the next
mighty steelhead, perhaps (always) the fish of a lifetime.

From there the river flows rapidly down a chute and past
a great logjam to crash against the left bank, a rock wall
with a deep hole at its foot bored out by the current. I sus-
pect that is where Ted will choose to ply his full sinking line
past the noses of waiting steelhead. Then the river slows as it
approaches another logjam and becomes a long, ambling run
holding fewer fish, but those that do hold there are looking
up, anticipating my fly. The suspense can be palpable.

Ted, like most Europeans, is almost paranoid about the
danger posed by bears. So I don't mention that only the week
before, on the spot we have chosen to fish, a long-time Dean
River aficionado was charged by a mother grizzly even as he
sprinted downstream fighting, according to his telling, the
"mother of all steelhead." He claimed it was the biggest he
had encountered in almost sixty years of angling. Refusing
to break off the fish, he kept running downstream until the
grizzly finally gave up the chase, rearing up on her hind legs
and roaring as she shook her shaggy head. I am not partic-
ularly nervous about bears, even having, as a youthful park
ranger, once surprised a bruin in my cabin; it made good
its escape by bursting through the back screen door, leaving a hole the size of a wheelbarrow. But it would be rather

unpropitious to have an incident involving *Ursus horribilis* and poet on his first steelhead outing.

We fish with dry flies. They require very aggressive fish; only those tempted to rise to the surface will respond to such a presentation, perhaps the most difficult but satisfying method of hooking the notoriously reluctant steelhead on the fly. "Like making love with the lights on," I explain to my companion. But several casts bring no surges from the depths, even as we hear more maddening whoops from our companions dredging the river bottom. They're using Squamish Poachers—prawn imitations that Joe Kambeitz, a relentless and skilled former bait fisher, concocted out of bright orange surveyor's tape; they are disdained by salmon fly purists, company not including Ted and me.

"Enough is enough. Put on a sinking tip line and a Squamish Poacher, and I shall put on a Davie Street Hooker"—a polar bear hair, silver and pink pattern of my own concoction that pays tribute to the beauty and perhaps inconstancy of Vancouver's ladies of the night. Ted's powerful meathook hands engulf the gaudy bauble he fastens to his leader. "Sometimes they just have their noses buried into the gravel, especially if they have been there awhile," I explain. "You have to bring the fly to them."

Ted lifts his powerful fifteen-foot Bruce and Walker rod and fires the fly into the current as I become the gillie, the hired man devoted to getting his client a fish. I am too engrossed in the efforts of my charge to fish myself.

"Turning off the lights, are we, Ehor?" Ted comments wryly.

"Afraid so," I say. "Better sex in the dark than none at all."

On the third cast, Ted's rod tip dips and he is into a lovely fish, not large (perhaps eight or ten pounds) but very silvery and aerial, hurtling itself out of the river six or seven times before he brings it to shore. In Europe, salmon fishing is about killing fish, and I watch anxiously as he unhooks the fish and, panting rapidly, crouches to admire it, repeating in a kind of thanksgiving mantra: "Thank you, Ehor, thank you, for bringing me to my first steelhead. She is surpassingly beautiful. Thank you." And then, unprompted, cradles it with his forearm, pointing it into the current until it frees itself of his grasp and disappears.

I heard twigs crack in the dark forest while Ted was fighting the fish, and now a rancid, musky odour permeates the area. Miz Grizz is back. "Come, Ted," I murmur. "Let's rest this pool," and I whisk him into the raft. I hear a low grunt behind me but make no mention until we reach the far shore. Ted is happy, oblivious.

· · ·

THE TRIP IS the culmination of a five-month process that began with a series of letters back and forth, laying out our plans. Ebullient after our evening together, I proposed Ted· join friends in a scheme to fish different rivers across the country. Tasked with choosing a B.C. river, I had in mind the Dean, during the several weeks in the summer when my fishing club mounts its annual expedition. While I was posting my original invitation to him, Ted was writing me. He enclosed a beautiful little book of poems and pointed out one in particular—"Saint's Island"—set on Lough Ree wherein the mayflies that hatch on the lake alight on the trees then descend onto the leeward waters of the island, where giant trout cruise like plankton-filtering whales, inhaling millions while the anglers wait in boats, ready to place a fly just in front of the cruising behemoths. He ended his letter by saying he could be in Vancouver by August 15 and that his brain had turned to mush, having spent a year and two hundred thousand dollars battling the allegations of the woman who imagined herself portrayed in Sylvia's novel.

Delving into the book, Ted's *Flowers and Insects*, I was charmed by poems about daffodils and bees, but most by the aforementioned "Saint's Island," dedicated to his friend Barrie Cooke, a wonderful artist who chose to live in Ireland because of the fishing. The poem is indeed about the mayfly, that most delicate and beautiful aquatic insect—"monstrous, but tiny" in Ted's words—that is dearest to the heart of the flyfisher.

I fished a mayfly hatch only once. They poured from the water like an inverse yellow snowstorm on a remote lake on Nova Scotia's Eastern Shore. That experience was intense, but as a neophyte flyfisher, I concentrated on the miracle of actually catching good-sized fish at will. I was back to being a child, hooking walleye on bait in Red Lake. Ted, for his part, looked beyond the purely carnal to the utterly amazing phenomenon of the hatch of minuscule, ethereal (even their genus is named *Ephemeroptera*) creatures behind the experience.

What I learned about Ted from this and subsequent letters was how passionate he was about every aspect of fishing, from catching to conservation and, like every true enthusiast, even about the equipment of fishing, which is ever-improving, with ever more specialized instruments filling increasingly rarefied niches and creating an insatiable need in the fly angler perhaps rivalled only by a stylish woman's lust for shoes.

On May 1 Ted wrote to inform me that he had passed my article on spey rods published in *Fly Rod and Reel* to Conrad Voss Bark, a writer and broadcaster who had become very well known during the war. He in turn had written an article for *The Times* of London about it: the B.C. long-rod revolution. Ted then went on to describe how bemused the locals in Alaska had been to see Nick's and his wielding of mere eleven-foot double-handers. He described his armamentarium to include two fifteen-foot Bruce and Walkers, that eleven-footer and an odd-lengthed ten-foot, six-inch number that he claimed was the more powerful of the two. Fishermen love the craftwork of their passion, from rods to reels to flies, to a degree beyond devotees of any other sport I have encountered, and clearly Ted was no exception. He described how sadly slow fishing was and how the Torridge, a beautiful but badly polluted local river, was adopted by Greenpeace as its "mascot" to highlight water pollution in England. He ended by underlining his mounting excitement regarding his upcoming visit to British Columbia.

Finally in late August I pick Ted up at the airport and bring him to my Irish friend John Hamill's bachelor party at Ioanni's Greek restaurant. John is concerned about an effete upper-class English artiste casting a pall on the festivities, but when Ted arrives, hulking, craggy, jetlagged and gently friendly, John is relieved: "He's just a big old farmer in a burgundy cardigan. I like him already." When I tell Ted on the drive to Deep Cove, he is pleased at the characterization and goes on to describe his years working with his wife Carol's father on his Devon farm, of the beautiful champion bull they had. It was that period that inspired the fine collection *Moortown*. We exchange rapid-fire stories of fish and rivers and farms and writing and children, and by the time I pull into the driveway, he is asleep.

The next day, we shop for the last bits of wine and Scotch—most of the nonperishables and booze are awaiting us at the Bella Coola airport some five hundred kilometres north, several hours west of Williams Lake by road. It is the end of that road. From there we have to fly to the Dean Channel, the next fiord. But at the moment, we have a major problem. Vicky is leaving for Scotland for her grandparents' sixtieth wedding anniversary and asks me to write a poem. I am packing feverishly for the Dean and getting ready for John's wedding while working on the poem. I have an idea

about the confluence of Celt (Sam McGinn) and Viking
(Mary Haste) flowing to the sea and to far shores, etc. I ask
Ted to help, given the short time. "Just say what you want to
say, as simply as you can," he advises. I write a draft, revise
it and he takes it and edits the last draft. Within an hour we
have "For Mary and Sam," which he writes out longhand for   *31*
us and Vicky goes on to read at the party:

> Sixty Summers ago
> Veins of Viking and Celt
> Conflowed,
> And the River McGinn
> enriched the earth
> Winding through the hills of
> Kilmacolm.
> The eddies flowered, offspring strong
> and rooted
> Lifted heads of auburn and gold
> Marrying stream and bank.
> Winds of passing seasons
> Sowed their seed over the spring
> currents.
> The river's mouth
> Gave them to the Atlantic.
> They drifted to a world new and old,
> Threading unknown rivers,
> Sinking roots in unfamiliar eddies

Where seeds gathered from many lands
Mingled their strengths, and flowered
Afresh
Lifting again heads of gold and auburn.
Now September winds bend them
towards the home shore
Remembering the parent's dream
Which still gleams among the
home hills.

That night we celebrate the nuptials of John and his bride, Cathy, at a charming garden wedding service and party at which I am flattered to serve as best man. Ted looks rather striking in my sky-blue silk jacket and despite his fatigue appears to be at ease, every bit as gracious as on that first night at UBC's Recital Hall. He is obviously enjoying himself immensely, exploring a strange and, perhaps to him, somewhat unselfconsciously ingenuous culture. Here he is not the Poet Laureate but merely my friend from England.

Vicky drives us to the airport as the first sunbeam bursts over the North Shore mountains and bathes the city in a warm amber glow. Tired from the celebrations of the previous night, we have had our final showers and shaves for a week. On the tarmac we are greeted by Jay Rowland, the wry-witted and somewhat acerbic fisherman I met eleven years before at an Osprey Flyfisher Club dinner. Despite our very different personalities, we became close friends. And

Ron Cordes, a well-spoken, modulated, but very competitive and achievement-oriented American. Ron possesses both a PhD in engineering and a JD in law and, as I've discovered over several trips to the Dean, is a great storyteller obsessed with catching as many steelhead as possible.

We board a yellow and white twin-engine Navajo, pungent with the odour of old leather, worn rubber and aircraft fuel. The dinky seats appear constructed for Kentucky Derby jockeys rather than hulking professors and poets, but we strap ourselves in and watch the world recede, a radiant city nestled on the sea before a massive fortress of mountains running north and south behind it. The two-and-a-half-hour flight over the coastal range reveals the Chilcotin below us. As the crow flies, the region is just over the mountains from Vancouver, yet it remains one of the most remote and untrod parts of British Columbia. In the brilliant sunshine it glows as one of the earth's great unfolding spectacles of island-dotted azure Pacific fiords, undulating icefields, broad river valleys and shardlike mountaintops.

Ted's face is aglow, and he keeps chuckling to himself. We swoop down into the airport in the Bella Coola River valley, a surprisingly flat, well laid-out area in the river's flood plain, overseen by Nusatsum Mountain shimmering in the morning sunshine like a Nepalese fortress rising some eight thousand feet into the sky. Told we have a two-hour wait, we commandeer a half-ton pickup, and with Ron and me bouncing in the box, we track down a restaurant on the road to Hagensborg. It is the kind of tired plywood-and-clapboard structure ubiquitous in the Canadian bush. The fresh-faced young waitress who brings us our logger's breakfasts of sausages, eggs, bacon, toast and dishwater coffee is the daughter of Felix, the recluse who used to live at Kimsquit and transport anglers to the upper river in his battered truck. She's certainly no longer the scruffy barefoot urchin I remember. Back at the airport, our group is to split, with two people taking the helicopter and a few supplies. Ted is keeping his feelings under wraps but is excited at the prospect of a helicopter trip. After loading both aircraft in the blazing noon sun, we pause in amazed silence that it all fits: no backpackers' special, this expedition.

Jay graciously suggests that Ted and I take the helicopter into camp. I can hardly contain my elation: paydirt! He and Ron will follow on the more prosaic fixed-wing flight, bearing most of the camp provisions. I pour my two-hundred-and-thirty-pound frame into the minuscule backseat of the Bell Jet Ranger, which is as parsimoniously designed and seemingly as fragile as a giant dragonfly. Ted overflows the seat next to the pilot, headphones perched on his thick, dark thatch, smiling broadly through clenched teeth: the picture of fear and excited anticipation. Our conversation is buried in a whine that turns to a roar and, somewhat uncannily, the entomological wonder is magically airborne, the earth, Jay and Ron increasingly diminutive below.

The pilot is a nervous perfectionist (not a bad thing in a chopper pilot). He takes us past gawking mountain goats blissfully munching greenery on mossy ledges suspended thousands of feet above the valley bottom, past great craters and the geological wreckage of strata pushed skyward in fanciful formations. Ted turns to me, grinning broadly, eyes blazing.

And then we sweep over the ridge and suddenly far below is the river of a thousand dreams. From Anahim Lake the Dean flows as a lovely trout stream rich with limestone, brimming with insect life, meandering through forest and meadow. As it threads through the coastal range, it picks up strength and colour from glacially fed tributaries, its character becoming wilder, fiercer and more powerful. Below us the alchemy is complete and we careen over a mighty river, charging in serpentine splendour to the sea, slowing occasionally into broad reaches, pools and runs that seemingly shift moment to moment from obsidian to chartreuse as sun and cloud alternate their conjury.

"My God, it's even more beautiful than I imagined," gasps Ted. "What a magnificent river! And look at that!" As our chopper hurtles at treetop level upstream, a mother grizzly and her two cubs, visions of shimmering, liquid bronze, break into a lope at a pace that would challenge a thoroughbred. Suddenly, they halt and stand gazing at us, mum with one paw raised as if in greeting, though we know better.

It is almost too much, and the cheerful tarps and tents of the Totem campsite glowing orange and blue are a calming sight as we bank to land. Our site is on a high cutbank overlooking the prime Home Pool—where seemingly every steelhead will pause for a day or two on its prematrimonial journey to its natal spot on the river. There is a clearing of perhaps an eighth of an acre with a copse of cottonwoods, willows and trembling aspen, just enough space for a large tent and kitchen area under a sheltering tarp and a landing spot for the chopper. Waiting for us on the ground are Lee Straight, late of *The Vancouver Sun* and the dean of Canadian outdoor editors; his son Ron, an ambulance professional; retired Canadian general Paul Smith, who is a college buddy of Lee's; and Canadian hockey legend Howie Meeker, he of the "Did you see that?" expostulation from the Soviet-Canada Summit series of 1972.

We hear stories of their mixed fishing success. Lee in his understated style reports "okay fishing." Anywhere else in the world, the fishing would be characterized as extraordinary. They hooked forty, landing twenty over the seven days. I surreptitiously watch Ted who, trying to take in the river, the mountains, the helicopter ride, the stories and the place that we will call home for seven days, is weaving about nearly inebriated from sensory overload.

The river is almost unprecedented in its clarity and low flow. Bags are hurriedly unpacked, and Jay insists we split wood and lay the fire before we fish, citing "Last Cast" Boyanowsky's reluctance to leave off fishing even as the sun is setting. Finally, with groceries unpacked, iceboxes hefted by pulleys out of reach of our furry friends, we are allowed to assemble our gear. Strange how simple tasks such as pulling on waders, tying laces and stringing up rods are beset with difficulty when the angler trembles in anticipation of that first cast. At long last we are ready and, as Ron and Jay slide effortlessly into the current below camp, Ted and I push our way through a thicket of underbrush and vicious thorns, willows and clinging, foot-snagging roots to attack the water.

We return to camp as the light disappears over the mountaintops, weary from casting and, thankfully, from fighting some very fine fresh-run steelhead. The initial anxiety ("Will we catch any fish at all?") is assuaged, which is no light matter: one club member came for two years running without hooking a steelhead. In the dying twilight, Ted sits in his camp chair looking like a great unmade bed, pausing in his struggle to get his second foot out of waders that cling to his legs with gluelike persistence from the accumulated perspiration. His thick black hair is matted to his forehead, yarmulke-like around his crown, and a spray of sweat flies off his face as he struggles with the infernal rubber membrane encasing him. He reminds me of a metamorphosing stonefly, struggling out of its husk. But there is a broad smile on his face. He accepts a glass of Macallan without removing his gaze from the mountaintops.

The mood is shattered by Jay's astringent orders: "Okay, you airy-fairy poetic types, let's get this dinner going! Ehor, put out the appetizers. Ted, light the fire. Ron, get the camp lantern going. C'mon, guys, it's going to be pitch dark in fifteen minutes!" We spring into action as the chef barks out the orders, and his grand plan for dinner unfolds. That night we celebrate with our annual first night's feast of fresh seafood, a tradition begun partly as sybaritic devotion, partly in cheeky affront to the mentality that presumes camping dictates a menu of macaroni, dried foods and sliced white bread. Toasts of Macallan and Glenmorangie malt whisky are hoisted in honour of each fish, especially that first steelhead of Ted's. He appears pleased with his initiation into the select group of anglers who have taken a wild steelhead on the fly, having landed not one but two in his first day's effort.

Ted turns to me: "Ehor, the strange thing is I had already lived today, thanks to you."

"What do you mean?"

"It was just like one of the poems you sent me, about the shooting stars."

I flush with surprise and pleasure that my poem has done a little for him what so many of his have done for me. My friends urge me to recite "The Perseids Run":

> It prowls the depths inciting violence
> And the cavalier connects with a new reality
> A second miracle is bestowed.
> Night descends in delicious exhaustion.
> We laugh, we eat
> We lie our backs on the cool sand
> Sharing the celebration of the skies
> In a shower of cascading stars.

"Everything but the Perseids themselves, Ted," I say with a laugh. For the meteor showers themselves, you have to be here earlier, in mid-August.

The next day dawns a sodden grey but rewards us with great fishing. It ends, however, with an unrelenting downpour that swells the river to a molten lava–like torrent, and for the next two days we are camp-bound, reduced to eating, drinking, tying flies and telling stories amid the hiss and clatter of the monsoon. Ted delights in relating ghost stories with a compelling raconteurship that has the hair on the nape of the usually curmudgeonly Jay's neck standing on end. It begins as the purple twilit mountain horizon darkens to an infinite abyss behind the crackling flames of the huge fire we keep stoking in the rain. Ted hunkers down in the chair, his earflapped Mongol goatherd's chamois hat encasing everything but his Roman nose and dark, burning eyes. He picks up a mug of coffee laced with Scotch, sips at it and in a sonorous voice starts exploring all the animal, spiritual and universal mysteries that fascinate him. He describes a meeting with a horse on a rain-lashed Devon moor that obviously intimidated and even spooked him, becoming grist for a haunting short story. Although not a pure ghost story, it typifies his view that nature is neither completely knowable nor completely sinister. Even *The Iron Man,* which began as a bedtime story for his children and in publication went on to become a favourite English children's book, is a tale of the struggle between the forces of nature and the constructed realities of humanity: in Hughes's view, an unwinnable battle.

His favourite poltergeist is the young girl who appears in a nightgown at the foot of the bed in one of his guest rooms, sometimes beckoning the bemused now-awakened slumberer to follow her downstairs. Ted wishes she would appear to him so that he might follow her, as no one's ever had the courage to do before. "I believe ghosts are troubled spirits, usually not too distant in the past, who need some tragedy reconciled."

Ted describes with deep conviction the work of water diviners and healers, those who can cure merely by a laying-on of hands. I realize my new friend's psyche dwells a good part of the time in the land of spirits and shadows.

We decide to have Ted serve as recording secretary for the week's adventures in the Totem camp logbook, a task the newest member of the group is usually asked to undertake. We all take turns dictating as he dutifully scribbles. A nobler role than the one he will eventually inherit in the spectrum of camp duties.

Week beginning August 29, 1987

For all of us, this was a week of extreme lows and extreme highs. The outgoing team left us with a luxuriously furnished camp but only average hopes of fish. Veterans had only once seen the river lower.

Even so we began with a bang: Ron and Jay had a double in Victoria Run before Ehor and Ted had

uncoiled their fifteen foot rods or launched Thompson
River Rats. At the end of this first day eight fish landed
out of thirteen hooked were celebrated with Glenmorangie Malt, four live lobsters, white Garlic Bread and
Salad, washed down with Sumac Ridge Verdelet—this
last item having been chilled in a monumental booze-
cache, designed and built by Ehor in the river shallows.
By next morning the surprises had started and they
didn't let up till we left. Gusty night wind had brought
rain and squally dragging cloud, with the river up three
inches and still rising. But the fish were excited. Jay got
a fifteen pounder in Cub Run on a dry fly, and another
of 35 1/2 inches in Totem Pool, where Ron lost a 'giant
fish'. Ted had caught his first ever Steelhead yesterday when he switched to sunk fly, and now he started
hooking them in the top of Victoria. One that he lost
was, according to Ehor who was trying to photograph
it being beached, 'the biggest fish I've ever seen caught
on the Dean'—estimating it upwards of 25 lbs before
it kicked off on the stones. Then Ehor had a phenom-
enal hour in the tail-out of the Victoria. In front of an
audience of Fishermen he had over 30 rises to his River
Rat, hooking four of them, one a giant, before the glacial milk arrived and the still-rising river went dead.
The rest of that day we sat under the stormy tarp, with
pans flying round our ears, watched the cataract braids
thicken on the mountain face opposite, saw a Grizzly

going down the opposite bank, feasted on spicy chicken
and stir-fry vegetables and forgot our gloom under vol-
umes of wine with the labels flooded off.

The next three days were almost totally washed out.
That Monday morning the water was still coming up,
creamy with ice-melt, and an unnaturally warm wind
promised more. We see-sawed all that day between long
sessions sitting in prayer under the tarp and short spells
fishing in vain. We recovered on Steak with Bearnaise
Sauce, Baked Potatoes and magnums of unnamed red.

The following day, Tuesday the 1st, spirits went
down as the river came up and up. This was the day we
almost cracked. Rapids above were a great foggy boil
of milk, and the rain heavy off and on all day. Guide
boats came down for the first time today, and after sitting under the tarp gorging on Jay's glorious pancakes
and watching those boys fishing in misery for a couple
of hours we finally went out to share it, just for the exer-
cise. Ron and Jay didn't go far, so they were there to
see a Black Bear stroll into the Camp for an inspection.
They managed to eject him without firing a shot, but
then he wandered upriver and came out two rod lengths
from Ted, who was fishing near Ehor below Fir Tree
run. That afternoon the river rose four feet till the tip
sweeper of the logjam ploughed water. A group camping downriver lost hope and pulled out. This was the
nadir. But Ehor reminded us of the great fishing they'd

been getting below the gorge, as we'd heard. As we sat there trying to feel optimistic, four morose German Kayakers went past. They'd come all the way from Nimpo Lake yet they wouldn't stop for a coffee. Later we learned their fifth member had been drowned three days upriver. A dead Black Bear sailed past at dusk.

Wednesday the 2nd dawned with a bright cold sky and the river already down about a foot. This was a beautiful day to waste time. We walked to the bridge, saw the dead Black Bear beached on the shingle island below Victoria Run, found plentiful signs of deer, bear and wolf. All through the afternoon Steelhead were showing near shore opposite Camp as the river fell rapidly, and the white streaks up the mountains shrivelled to near nothing. When Ehor's cromlech bottle cellar became dimly visible in the clearing water we started to fish, and Ehor and Ted hooked several Steelhead very close inshore opposite the logjam. So our spirits were soaring that night as we lowered the Malt, ate Barbecue Steaks, a huge Greek salad and washed all down with Sumac Ridge Chancellor.

Thursday dawn we dashed out breakfastless to beat the Guide boats, but even so before Ted and Ehor could get clear of the Camp Ron was into a Steelhead opposite. By evening we'd landed 15 out of 21, and Jay had had his best Steelhead day ever. The Camp Mice ran up our arms and over the table and sat round the fire with us that night celebrating. Next day, Friday, was even more productive. By noon we'd landed 12 out of 17, all in the Totem pool or Victoria, but then under a very bright sun the fish lost interest. Then towards evening the river woke up again for all of us. Ron and Jay started catching Steelhead on request for the Fishery boys to tag opposite the logjam and Camp; Ehor was hustled from the Camp logjam right down through Victoria by a sixteen pounder; Ted caught several in the neck of Victoria—two of them after dark. This was the week's top day, 21 fish landed out of 28 hooked, with Ron equalling his best day ever.

Even Saturday morning, when we had to pack up the Camp, showed us what we were leaving. We had everything ready by ten, but in the next hour, before the helicopter arrived, Ted landed one in Victoria, Jay hooked three and landed two opposite the Camp logjam, and in the same place Ehor landed his smallest ever Steelhead—three pounds.

One of the great weeks. The three day wash-out spoiled the dry fly water. But it brought up all those new fish. And it gave the week a definite beginning, middle and end, which made everything more dramatic and intense. We landed some big ones (several near the 20 pound mark), and lost some very big ones, ending up with 54 out of 81.

It is clear that Ted used a copy that he made of our log entry as the model for "The Bear," which was included in the edition of *River* republished in the volume *Three Books* in 1993:

> The day darkened in rain. In the bottom of the gorge   *45*
> The big tarp awning we sat approximately under
> Bucked in its ropes. Pans took off.
> Nothing we could do

In those few lines Ted captured the immediacy and the power of weather experienced as only those trapped by it in the wilderness, far from home, can appreciate. But the greatest fear is not of its power. Rather, for the angler who has dreamed of the trip for the best part of a year, and lived in anticipation of it, the prospect that it might be ending prematurely and very abruptly represents the ultimate tragedy:

> maybe this was The Rains—
> The winter coming early. Maybe the river
> Never would surrender Ehor's wine-cache
> Already four feet under the sliding concrete
> Till maybe next June

Of course, the mind races contemplating a solution. Ron, ever the American man of action, had immediately suggested calling in a chopper and heading back to Vancouver, where we could at least enjoy the restaurants, perhaps some sun, but most of all be liberated from the tyranny of the elements, the power of the raging god who so cavalierly toys with the outcome of our pilgrimage to this mecca of steelhead. I had tried to keep spirits bucked up by pointing out how the rise and drop in water levels will produce a wave of silver bright, fresh steelhead surging from the sea and so:

> we sat there
> And enjoyed it. And the Steelhead down there
> They were enjoying it too, this was what they were
>   made of,
> And made by, and made for, this was their moment.

Ted's lines are a brilliant demonstration of how a poem distills the mundane and extraordinary events described by four men into a moment that glows forever. That's the poem that came out of our log entry, but during the surge of high water Ted worked on another poem—"The Black Rhino"—that he offered at auction in a benefit for the great beast in London. It was published in *The Daily Telegraph* that October.

Lee is on the tarmac to greet us in Vancouver and to pick up the camp gear we are returning as the last group of the year.

"Well, how was the fishing?" he inquires. As we tell him stories of the riches we encountered, he cuts us off with:

"What do you consider hooked? More than a pull, I hope? Was every landed fish witnessed?" Exasperated, we show him the camp log. "I will have to examine this and get back to you," he retorts, ever the skeptical newspaperman. "Stories are marginally more credible if they are in writing. Got pictures?" I roll my eyes but can scarcely hide my affection.

Back in Deep Cove, we scrape off a week's mantle of camping grit and grease, adjust to central heating and wander about reliving the week with Vicky and friends who call. After a day of mostly hanging out, napping and chatting, playing music (Ted loves traditional Celtic and mediaeval music, hates jazz) we wander over to the Dollarton section of Deep Cove to ply the beaches for foraging cutthroat with tiny No. 4 and 5 single-handed rods. After the mighty steelhead of the Dean, fishing for twelve- to eighteen-inch cutthroat with a fairy wand appears somewhat Lilliputian, but Ted is enjoying himself, waist deep in the ocean, slitted eyes scanning the velvet surface for the telltale dimple of a feeding fish. When he lands his first, he kneels in the shallows cupping the little golden trout as gently as he would a baby.

It is late evening and Ted, Vicky, Alexei, my teenage daughter Thea and I are sitting on our balcony. Given this location and V's propensity for breastfeeding here, I explain that one of Alexei's first words was "bird," another "moon," and Ted responds with a similar story about his daughter, Frieda, whom he raised along with Nicholas after their mother's death. Ted was vilified for years after Sylvia

Plath's suicide, an act she'd previously attempted as a teenager. He never defended himself publicly. When I ask why
he married her, given her tortured personality, he responds:
"Because she was beautiful, passionate, a genius and I loved
her." When I ask why he hasn't written poems about her, he
says he has but that out of consideration for his present wife,
Carol, who is the centre of his life, he won't publish them. (In
1998 he finally will in *Birthday Letters*, to enormous critical
and popular acclaim, putting to rest forever accusations that
he was callous in their relationship.) Ted again tells the story
of overhearing wolves howling at the nearby London Zoo,
one of the many places he worked after leaving Cambridge.
Ted feels those primary, if not primal, experiences shape the
psyche of a child and, as a psychologist, I cannot disagree.
I tell Ted I will show him where his countryman Malcolm
Lowry wrote *Under the Volcano*, but he claims not to know
either the author or the work. He explains that he has paid
little attention to novels, regarding them as inflated poems.
Every novelist he knows wrote his first successful book when
he was desperate for money and couldn't think of anything
else to do, he says.

We watch the evening sky fill with light. Alexei raises his
hand and points in the silence that has engulfed the group.
"Moon," he says.

We go inside and I put on the 1976 National Film Board
documentary *Volcano* by Donald Brittain. It tracks Lowry's life from his boyhood in England to his seafaring, his

binge drinking in Mexico and his days writing *Under the Volcano* in nearby Dollarton. It is a powerful and beautiful film. Ted's voice crackles with enthusiasm as he talks about the literary isolation of England, of how he tries to promote more interaction with European poets and how he laments his self-imposed estrangement, until now, from cultural North America.

3 / ART ON THE THOMPSON

The bond among those who fish goes beyond the passion for merely catching the most or the biggest. Anglers tend to relate best to other anglers who share their values. It's not enough to catch the most fish, even of the most difficult or rarest species. Those who continue in perpetuity to be happy merely using natural bait exclusively rather than challenging themselves by rising to artificial lures and eventually flies (preferably ones that they have tied and even designed themselves), I eventually relegate to the status of accountant. They can say how many fish are in the river and may be expert anglers but suffer from a case of arrested development or hidden anatomical deficiencies of such gravity that they cannot countenance coming off the river empty-handed. I must confess there are even some prominent flyfishers who suffer from the same syndrome.

And so, there is a special delight in bringing together anglers who not only share in the joy of fishing, but discover larger pleasures and passions as well. This is one such story.

I am standing in a flat-bottomed pram that is little more than a casting platform on a mountaintop lake called Peter Hope. With its crystalline water and shimmering white marl shoals it is one of the most spellbinding and challenging of the myriad lakes in the Merritt area, sitting at 3,550 feet on the Guichon Ranch near the south end of Stump Lake. By now it is dark. I can barely see the dry fly—concocted to resemble a caddis, a.k.a. a traveller sedge, the prolific insect whose hatching on the surface triggers a trout feeding frenzy. I strip it in with short bursts along the shimmering glasstop surface as a giant silver moon mounts the horizon. Hearing is the paramount sense: the hiss of flylines, the violent splash of rainbows savaging the fly, the angry scream of the reel as a muscular Kamloops trout motors towards the bullrushes. Nighttime provides a cloak of anonymity. Revelations emerge that would not be offered in the glare of the afternoon.

From his soft-spoken responses to my queries, I learn my dusky-silhouetted neighbour, who is casting elegantly from a boat fifty metres away, lives on the lake, is an artist, grew up in Portugal with English and Spanish parents and, at the urging of his boyhood mentor, a former whaler called Francisco, came to British Columbia as a young man to embrace the dream he had discovered in the books of writers like Roderick Haig-Brown. When the hatch ends and the trout stop rising, he accepts an invitation to my cabin, where for the first time I see an El Greco visage, aquiline-profiled, blackbearded and topped by a black cowboy hat.

"You've learned more about me in a couple of hours than most people do in years," chuckles Ken Kirkby. By daybreak and most of a bottle of Scotch, we have become friends, discovering a love of the north country—mine Ontario, north of Thunder Bay; his the Arctic, where he lived for a few years with the Inuit. Over the next several years we will share a great number of adventures, hunting and fishing, but most of all sitting around the kitchen table, cooking dinner and waxing loquacious on a hundred topics. Usually we meet when he can visit from Toronto, where he moved to be near his son and to pursue his fortune selling his magnificent paintings of inukshuks: the striking "stone man" markers of the Inuit that have become the symbol of the Vancouver 2010 Winter Olympics.

When I describe Ted to him, Ken is keen to connect and plans to join us for a sojourn in the Thompson River valley whose landscape has captured my heart. Not that it was always so. When I first ventured out from the Coast I was repelled by the grittiness of its fierce and desolate aspect, a stark contrast to the verdancy of the Pacific.

Ted is returning to British Columbia in order to appear at an arts festival in Victoria, where he will give a reading and possibly participate in some shamanistic aboriginal ceremonies in a village farther up Vancouver Island. He is quite enthused because he has induced his grad-student son, Nicholas, to join us from Fairbanks. When I pick him up at the airport, though, Ted looks tired and worried. Apparently he has been told that he will be meeting a Queen Elizabeth impersonator on stage during his presentation and he is concerned lest the London tabloids get hold of it and make him out to be mocking the monarch. The queen has already incurred some criticism for appointing him, his being a rather unconventional choice given his less than completely accessible poetry. For the first time, Ted refers to his position with the royal family, revealing that he takes his laureate duties seriously and, tabloids aside, he does not want to engage in anything that smacks of ridicule.

Vicky, Ted and I walk down from Lookout Point to the Nutshell, a charming French restaurant on the water in Deep Cove. The ocean and surrounding mountains are bathed in the soft mauve and cerise glow of twilight as we pad down the hikers' trail among the giant cedars and Douglas firs. Ted is exhausted but animated. He is also sadly agitated by the predicament in which he finds himself; as I increasingly discover, he is loath to disappoint anyone for whom he cares or sympathizes. Sitting in the Nutshell, we sip a fine burgundy while staring through candlelight at the dusk gathering over Indian Arm. On the walk back he decides to refuse the impersonator business, but there is no sense of relief about his manner. He is perspiring profusely. Vicky suggests he choose not to attend at all and just come for a longer trip with us to the Thompson, but he dismisses that cut-and-run solution out of hand.

On my way out to lecture the next morning, I knock on his door and he groans that he has a touch of indigestion. He reluctantly accepts some Alka-Seltzer, and I tell him I will call from the university. I am a bit puzzled, as we all ate the same entrée, but he, after all, just completed a nine-hour flight replete with airline food, so it makes some sense that his system might be out of whack. When I do call, his voice is barely recognizable, so I cut short my office hours, call Vicky to pick up Ken and Nicholas and race back to the house.

Ted tries to put on a brave face. He insists that all he needs is a spot of tea. While serving it, I ask him to lift his shirt and I take the liberty of poking the right side of his abdomen. He lets out a startled moan. We immediately head for the hospital, and within minutes he is decked out in a green nightshirt when Dr. Nick Marionatis, a well-regarded surgeon who has also done some work on me, shows up. A couple more pokes, an X-ray, and he announces Ted has an appendix on the verge of bursting. Marionatis, making small talk on the way, asks Ted what he does for a living. Ted offers that he "scribbles." Marionatis asks him what he means, and Ted answers that he is a writer.

"What sorts of things?"

"Different things," Ted responds, telling me later no one believes him if he says he writes poetry for a living.

A couple of hours later, as Vicky and I sip wine and

munch cheese with Ken and Nicholas, safely arrived from Toronto and Fairbanks, respectively, the phone rings. It is Ted. To our collective relief he sounds amazingly well. Despite the late hour, we troop over to see him. He is apologetic and attributes the alleged blockage to peanuts he ate on the plane. I don't go so far as to suggest that he willed the appendicitis upon himself, but it's certainly true that now he can beg off the Victoria trip. Nicholas—a handsome, quiet young man with an uncanny resemblance to his mother—says: "Well, Dad. No use our hanging around here. We're heading for the Thompson while you recuperate. There are fish to be caught." Much as he loves his dad, Nicholas has a pragmatic bent, as well as a special relationship with fish, wanting to catch any that exist in every pond or puddle he comes across—a born fisherman. Ted says that he will come up as soon as he is capable of travel, and Vicky promises to bring him in a few days.

The conversation on the road to the Thompson is good. Ken regales us with stories of growing up hunting and fishing in Portugal and then in British Columbia and the Arctic. Nick seems especially interested when Ken describes how he needed fifty thousand dollars to invest in property in order to finance his art career but when the bank turned him down (what—finance a twenty-one-year-old with no collateral?) he headed north, first working on the Peace River dam, then heading even farther north to live with the Inuit and to begin painting the inukshuks that eventually founded his career.

Nick asks a lot of questions and appears keen to experience more of the region and to fish for the enigmatic inconnu and Arctic char. He talks about growing up with Ted's second wife, Carol (née Orchard), whom he refers to as his mother, and going to boarding school, which he appears to have enjoyed, though it was a school of a somewhat counterculture variety with both boys and girls as residents. He even makes oblique references to his biological mother, though Ted has told me he never mentions Sylvia. He seems concerned about his dad, noting that in the past few years Ted has slowed down so that their excursions afield, to Ireland, Scotland and Iceland, have physically tamed a bit.

On the Thompson it is a time of diamond-bright days that crackle with the desperate energy of summer's last gasp. Nick is fascinated with the striking beauty of the arid Thompson River valley, commenting like many before him that it is not what he expected in British Columbia. The Thompson is the northern tip of the Great Basin Desert, which originates in Mexico and makes its way in the rain shadow of the Coast Mountains through Osoyoos to its northern terminus near Kamloops. The alchemy of alkaline water, heat and sparse rainfall (fifteen centimetres annually at Ashcroft) produce a climate that grows the sweetest corn and tomatoes in creation, nurtures many wildlife species including bighorn sheep and giant mule deer, and is home to especially ferocious aboriginals who, according to Annie Dillard in her 1992 novel, *The Living*, used to venture as far south as what is now Washington state in order to skewer the local tribes-people just to see how long their agony would last.

It is home, as well, to the reason for our journey. Our hopes of encountering the mighty steelhead are high. Word is out that an American lure company rep has landed and killed a thirty-two-pounder through the ignominious method of "hotshotting"—backing a boat slowly down-stream while dangling a vibrating lure from the transom, practically feeding it into the open mouth of a holding steel-head. The Thompson faithful are incensed and, amazingly (for they are notoriously lacking in the will to oppose any specific form of exploitation, for example the use of deadly bait such as roe), the provincial Fisheries Branch quickly bans fishing from boats.

We, however, are less fortunate. A day and a half of fly-fishing over sixteen kilometres of river has produced some lovely rainbow trout but no steelhead. When Vicky arrives with Ted and Alexei in tow, it is clear that Ted's stitches won't allow his negotiation of the cobbles and currents, so we decide to walk the orchards instead, hunting for chukar par-tridge, a lovely, swift-flying and delicious import from the Hindu Kush bordering Pakistan and Afghanistan that has taken to the valley's desert habitat.

Ken, Nicholas, Ted and I walk abreast through the apple trees of the orchard at Hilltop Gardens where I rent a cabin. The farm, on one of the tablelands overlooking the river, is an oasis of greenery in a desolate landscape of sagebrush and cactus, gardens bursting with brilliantly crimson tomatoes and sweet corn on one side; on the other, trees heavy with Spartan and McIntosh apples brimming with sugar from the desert sun. Alexei traipses just ahead of us, glorying in his leadership of the pack: "The first walk of children is a broken fall," observes Ted. We approach a tomato patch just as a cloud of chukars, grey with orange breast feathers and ninja-turtle masks over their eyes, bursts at warp speed from the rich, fleshy fruit into which they had buried their heads. Nick scoops up Alexei as Ken opens fire with his Beretta over-and-under and I knock off a shot with my Fox side-by-side. Two chukars plummet to the furrows. Alexei's head is swinging from side to side trying to monitor the action, but he betrays no distress. We walk over and pick up the birds. Alexei is curious and quite excited. So too are Ted and Nicholas. I offer my gun to Ted: "I haven't done this for twenty years," he says, his voice alive with anticipation. Nicholas takes Ken's gun.

As we walk out of the tomato patch into the sage, a second flock flushes. Ted fires twice, and two birds careen out of the sky. We give him a cheer—a double on chukars is no ordinary thing. "Strange how it comes back to you," he enthuses, "the thrill, the blood lust." Nicholas fires, hits nothing but expresses his desire to try this again. He will go after ptarmigan in Alaska for certain now, he says. After an hour we walk back to the cabin with several chukars on our belts. To the horror of my Canadian friends, though I actually learned it from *Larousse Gastronomique,* I will hang them in a cool dark place in the British tradition, to tenderize for seven to ten days. It actually works: the flesh is always cool when I collect them and no maggots can be found if they are sequestered in a fly-free environment, usually my garage. The wait will be worth it. It has been a good afternoon. Alexei is mesmerized by the birds, keeps stroking them and making shooting noises. Clearly we are witnessing the making of a future hunter. Later that evening, around a dinner of fresh halibut steaks and wine and Thompson Valley corn and tomatoes, Ted describes coming across a wounded grouse on the Yorkshire moors with Sylvia, and how upon his instinctively twisting its neck, Sylvia shrieked in horror.

"It was like someone throwing water on you and bringing you out of a trance—I suddenly realized how it must have looked from her uninitiated perspective and felt a great dread. I have killed no birds since . . . until today."

With the Thompson off-limits, we decide to drive up into the mountains to Blue Earth Lake, an isolated tarn nestled in the slightly wetter ecology of the boreal forest above the sagebrush line. The circuitous, almost Byzantine route along old logging roads delivers a wide spectrum of wildlife: bear, grouse, huge mule deer and even one bobcat that stares at us curiously as we drive by. Sagebrush gives way to sparse ponderosa pine set in parklike terrain and finally to impenetrable thickets of lodgepole pine. Turning a corner we encounter a glowing mirage of lapis lazuli and pause, taking in the mountaintop remoteness of the place, the wind moaning in the trees. An urgency to get out on the lake overtakes us. As we pump up our raft, the high-pitched, spine-tingling scream of a mountain lion echoes among the peaks of the crater lake. "In some ways, this is more wilderness than the Dean," Ted marvels, "and yet only a few miles from the main highway." Vicky and I fish from shore while Ted and Ken row out in the lake. Each of them hooks a fine fat rainbow on a dragonfly nymph fished deep, and when they pull to shore Ted is beaming, as pleased with these plump sixteen-inchers as he was with a sixteen-pound Dean River steelhead. Ken and he have been chatting incessantly, and the growing affection between them is evident as we descend back into the twilit valley.

As Vicky puts Alexei to bed and Nick retires to an early night, Ken, Ted and I drive into Spences Bridge, the little community of less than two hundred that each year plays host to a grand pilgrimage of steelheaders from around the world. Amazingly, it has not one but two destinations: the Steelhead Inn, one of the oldest continuously operating hotels in British Columbia; and the Log Cabin Pub, a giant log structure that is the watering hole of choice for cowboys, Indians, railroaders and anglers ready to laugh and scratch and trade lies about the day's events over a beer. Its interior is dimly lit and cavernous, with great logs for walls and even larger beams and posts underpinning the vaulted roof. Against the far wall, a large cast iron box stove lies dormant, awaiting the late autumn chill to spring into action. We sit below a snarling mountain lion condemned by the taxidermist's art to stalk the bar forever as the clink of glasses, the chortle of a waxing fishing raconteur's audience and the clacking of billiard balls combine into a cacophony of good fellowship. On the juke-box, Ian Tyson belts out "Summer Wages"—perfect. It is one of the few Interior cowboy bars I have frequented where I have never witnessed a fight. As we sprawl on our spindly chairs sipping jugs of Kootenay Mountain Ale, life feels good and Ted asks about the origins of the town. I recount how James Teit, a Scotsman, came to Spences Bridge in the 1880s as a young man to help at his uncle's general store but became very interested in the local aboriginal people, married a Shuswap woman and even championed their land claims in Ottawa. His greatest mark, however, was made in the publi-cation of ethnographies of the Interior Salish, and his collab-oration with the famous Columbia University anthropologist Franz Boas.

A wistful look enters Ted's eyes and he wonders out loud whether this was the place he dreamed about with his brother when they were boys: a land of cowboys and Indians and giant salmon. Ted's boyhood passion was reading cowboy comics filched from his parents' newsstand; his first major bit of verse, a bit of juvenilia in thumping tetrameter (the first of his collected poems) is "Wild West" and this setting conjures up its opening, of Carson McReared:

> Who, south of the 49th was feared
> Greater than any man ever before,
> And men went in fear of his .44 . . .

They made a pledge to emigrate but Gerald went to Australia and Ted ended up in Devon. Speaking of migration, Ted asks Ken how he ended up living in a fishing resort on Peter Hope Lake. Ken explains that he initially fished on the Coast, spending many days up the Squamish River and plying the beaches for cutthroat. Then he started exploring the Interior lakes—crystalline spring-fed ponds teeming with insect life, especially chironomids, caddis and gammarus, freshwater shrimp that promote the growth of huge rainbows wherever they are not overstocked with hatchery progeny. He enjoyed them all, but when he discovered Peter Hope he had an epiphany: here was home.

Eventually, he bought into a resort owned by a friend and, when his real-estate speculation business and his marriage imploded, he folded his tents and retreated to Peter Hope, which is where I found him. Ultimately, to be near his son, he followed his wife to Toronto, where he made his name and fortune with the inukshuk paintings for which he is increasingly known.

Talk turns to art. I ask Ted about his collaboration with Leonard Baskin, the highly esteemed artist and illustrator who did the wonderful pictures for Ted's books *Crow* and *Cave Birds*, and we start discussing our favourite artists. A very strange thing happens: Ted asks Ken and me to name our top three artists. Ken picks Hieronymus Bosch, Francisco de Goya and Lucas Cranach. The hair on the back of my neck stands erect, for those would be my three choices.

Ted is silent as I describe discovering Goya in a boyhood visit to the Art Gallery of Ontario, then Bosch in London and finally Cranach in books and various galleries.

"I can't believe this," Ted says in wonderment. "Those are my three choices as well." Ken's eyes are suddenly wet with tears. The conversation continues long after midnight, when we get back to the cabin. Coyotes yap and howl and, when we step outside, we are overwhelmed by an array of stars stretching from horizon to horizon, points of light cold and brilliant against a black velvet sky. To the north the aurora borealis is a swirling maiden in a feverish dance.

After Ted returns to Devon, I will ponder a great deal about what the three—Cranach, Bosch and Goya—have in common. Bosch was the earliest, born in 1450; Cranach was born in 1472, and we should also include his son, known as Lucas the Younger, for his work is regarded as indistinguishable from his father's. Goya, born three centuries later, painted many themes embracing the sacred and the profane in almost the same monstrous fashion as Bosch, as well as the exquisite image that many boys of my generation equated with female beauty and sex: *The Naked Maja.*

In the childhoods Ted and I had experienced, the main depictions of female nakedness available to our prurient curiosity were found in art galleries, exotic bare-bosomed maidens in *National Geographic* and Goya's nude woman, thought to be the Duchess of Alba. In her naked odalisque glory, she was always featured in the back pages of comic books on the famous stamp, *The Naked Maja*, to induce young boys to purchase stamps by mail order. Ted would have seen the ads; his family's newsagents shop in an industrial town in Yorkshire allowed a young Ted access to thousands of comic books. My older sister Lesia worked in a similar shop in our small Northern Ontario mining town and bought me comics regularly. Probing further in libraries, both Ted and I discovered the freakish wonders of Goya's art and its inevitable comparison by art historians to the frighteningly phantasmagorical creations of Bosch three centuries previous. But the shared attraction to the beauty and technique of Cranach, sparer and less carnal, remains a mystery.

Ken, by contrast, was raised in a wealthy family in Portugal and had an artist as his personal tutor. But he certainly shared our excitement at the mix of sex, violence and fantasy he discovered in galleries like the Prado in Madrid. Ken struck me as one of the gentlest, least violent people I had ever met but with an undercurrent of passion and anger that could be activated only with great provocation. He alluded to participation in the Portuguese revolution as a teenager, and of course he loved bird shooting. I also hunted and fished and, what's more, as a social and criminal psychologist, actually studied human aggression and violent crime and was the only one who had seriously played violent sports— hockey and Canadian football. But I see myself as relatively gentle as well, and in fact had been terrorized by a bully as a child, though I am more boisterous than the other two.

Ted appeared, if anything, the gentlest of us three. He had a passion for trapping and hunting as a boy, but unlike Ken's paintings, his poems deal often with violence and killing in the realm of fang and claw and, occasionally, their interception with human affairs. I recall the girl from "Crow's Song about England" whose mouth "was snatched from her and her face slapped," whose eyes "were knocked to the floor."

The next day, we wend our way back to Vancouver. When we get there, Ken presents Ted with a magnificent inukshuk oil painting. Ted protests, but Ken insists, convinced he has met a soul brother.

Perhaps the only thing better than meeting someone with whom you share a passion and a vision of the universe is to bring together two friends for whom you have great affection who would otherwise never meet, and see them connect and become fond of one another. It makes the universe expand suddenly and significantly. But it is a dangerous thing, for if they do not take to one another you may be forced to choose between them. It is a risk I will always regard worth taking and, as with the connection of the poet and the artist, it has led to some of the most gratifying experiences of my life. Love for the same three artists is not the only coincidence among us, however. We discover that the final common element that ignited our imaginations and drew us to British Columbia had been our reading, Ted's in Britain, Ken's in Portugal, mine in Northern Ontario, of the books of Roderick Haig-Brown, that British immigrant who had settled in Campbell River and went on to enthrall readers the world over with his stories of fishing the rivers of Vancouver Island.

LEFT: Ted arrives
on the Dean

BELOW: Ted hooks
his first steelhead

TOP: Ted, Vicky Mulholland and John Hamill at John's wedding

BOTTOM: Ted, Ken Kirkby and Nick holding Alexei

TOP: Ted and Nick with Chukars

BOTTOM: Nick with small steelhead on the Seymour River

TOP: Waiting out the storm: Ted, Rod Cordes and Jay Rowland

BOTTOM: Sacrificing the poet to the river gods

TOP: Ted and Ehor

BOTTOM: Dan Burns floating the Dean River back to the Totems' camp

TOP: Fighting a big one

BOTTOM: Releasing the big one

4 / HALCYON DAYS

Just like that, Ted has become an integral part of our lives. The literature in my field of social psychology concludes that very often caring for someone of some eminence inculcates a distancing resentment or at least a perfunctory expectation on their part. Less frequently, it cements an almost familial relationship. It feels like the latter is developing with Ted, and I'm delighted to see him reciprocate the feeling in the first letter after the Thompson trip.

Writing in October 1987, Ted reports that he is perfectly repaired thanks to the care he received in the crucial days of his malady. He mentions that if his bushy belly hair grows back to its original splendour the scar will be hardly noticeable and that he shall look as he feels—like a new beast. He appears concerned that I have never seen him completely hale and hearty and that I probably regard him as some kind of crippled creature but that in future he will be bounding from stone to stone footloose and fancy free, nailing fish in their holds. He recalls how endlessly patient we were and that he felt like Alexei, our infant son, with my holding the bowl and Vicky the spoon, while he awakened from a feverish dream to be nursed back to health. Ted ends by describing how the rhino poem he wrote on the Dean fetched thirteen hundred pounds at auction and that the fellow in charge who owns a fine piece of the Tweed (perhaps the most exclusive and expensive salmon river in Scotland) at Rutherford has extended an open invitation. He ends with a big kiss to Thea and "Alexeiviathan."

Already, I'm planning our second trip to the Dean with the same forethought that I'm applying to the whole year, a sabbatical one wherein I intend to carve out a new area in criminology: crimes against the environment. Central to it will be a visit to Haida Gwaii, the Queen Charlotte Islands, a remote archipelago populated by loggers, dropouts from society and proud, historically terrifying aboriginals, the Haida. And a trip to Ukraine, the land of my parents. Specifically Odessa, a sister city of Vancouver, as part of the official delegation from Vancouver's city hall. An important visit given the recent atomic catastrophe of Chernobyl.

I write to Ted of our plans for the new year and confirm the Dean trip. He responds in February with a breezy letter about the time flying by, whether Alexei is shouting "fish on" as he flings the cat like the hammer throw at the Highland Games and how he is struggling to get back to some serious work. He describes at some length the difficulty of making a career out of spinning out one's own entrails, comparing himself to a breeding female who knows what will emerge the first time but by the twentieth may produce a "warthog" or "an ice cream kiosk." He describes strange, fiendish weather, perhaps portending the collapse of the ecosystem with global warming, ozone depletion and the reversing of ocean currents. He laments how the rivers are open but no fish have shown up and the only good news is that, for the first time ever, the U.K. government has admitted national culpability in the production of devastating acid rain that originates in the clouds over power stations and damages trees, lakes and rivers beyond the responsibility of any other country in Europe. In passing he is pleased that the art dealer to whom he has shown Ken Kirkby's paintings is interested and that he shall be sending the contract regarding a fishing book that he and I plan to produce for Faber.

I am delighted to discover the depth of Ted's concern for the environment, which follows logically from his passion for fishing, for it is the human predator (the hunter, the fisher) who is most keenly aware of the state of the river. The evolved fisher knows the symbiosis between the insect life of a stream and the number of fish, small and large, that should be inhabiting it in different seasons. The telltale signs of health—weeds, but only the right kind; baby fish; stoneflies and caddis flies clinging to underwater rocks—are indices known only to those laypersons who have a passion to catch fish.

The issue of pollution is not merely theoretical for my family either. We are being forced to look for a new place to live, paradisiacal Deep Cove besmirched by pollution so acute that, given the public health advisory, our young son cannot even wade in the water on the beach at Panorama Park.

Searching for that ideal combination of wilderness, ocean and proximity to Vancouver, I wander down a former logging road, now a private residential lane in West Vancouver, on the outskirts of Horseshoe Bay: giant cedars create an otherworldly arboured sanctuary among which houses, slowly evolving from cottages to late-twentieth-century ostentatious architectural self-realizations, are nestled on the edge of a cliff. One modestly sized Richard Meier–like creation that resembles a mini-Moroccan fortress with its blank white walls facing the street is under construction right over, I take note, Hole in the Wall, a famous Howe Sound salmon fishing spot. Even in its unfinished state, it thrills me with its compact charm and proximity to the wooded point and little cove it overlooks. I'm sold.

The summer is a swirl of selling our house, closing on the new one, finding a contractor to finish it and preparing for the Ukraine and Dean trips.

At the end of the European visit, I am killing time in Heathrow Airport, still experiencing London culture shock but also savouring our amazing sojourn in Odessa, a city with an odd mix of the beautiful and unprepossessing Black Sea charm and inefficient Communist blandness. I'm hoping to get back to Vancouver before Ted who, I assume, is coming the next day. I am shaking my head at the surprise of picking up a copy of *TV Times* magazine off the news- stand and seeing my daughter, Jennifer Calvert (her stage name and her mother's family name, adopted after gradua- tion from London's Royal Academy of Dramatic Art when she couldn't get work as a Boyanowsky), on the cover, cour- tesy of *Brookside,* the popular television show in which she is appearing. Suddenly, a burly backpacker, a dark shock of silvertipped hair obscuring his face, enters my lineup. It is Ted. I can't believe our good fortune, as he doesn't have my phone number (nor in fact do I, the new house having been activated while I was abroad).

We end up sitting together, sharing bottles of wine and a few whiskies as Ted allows that he too was in a quandary about how to connect, but something—the mystic in him?— had assured him we would get together. On this flight, he avoids the peanuts. "Better safe than sorry. That would be like trying hanging twice."

We discuss our daughters. Ted is obviously very proud of Frieda and relieved that since "she has survived her rebel- lious years and come through relatively unscathed" she seems to have found her métier. (She has become an artist and poet herself; one of her paintings will grace the cover of the hardcover edition of *Birthday Letters,* the book in which

Ted finally breaks his silence on the subject of Sylvia's death.)
I express to him my concerns about what is happening to the
environment, especially given what I have seen in the USSR,
predicting it will trigger his own and I am not disappointed.

"It isn't just Russia. England seems determined to suf-
focate in her own swill: the factories are spewing out more
acid rain and, worse yet, more acid snow than any other
country in Europe to the point there are salmon streams in
Scotland too acidic to sustain baby fish and without them
the stocks are doomed, and the acid dissolving mercury and
other heavy metals in the stones in the streams is worsen-
ing an already bad situation." I am more than a little startled
by the vituperation expressed in this outburst and, glancing
sideways at Ted, I am amazed and gratified to see his eyes
glowing like burning coals, his mouth a grim slash in a reso-
lute jaw. He takes a sip of the Glenmore and opens his mouth
to continue but ends up just taking another sip and shaking
his head. His voice deepens even as it quiets to a harsh whis-
per: "In the south, in Devon where I live, some agricultural
bureaucratic geniuses have been encouraging farmers to
switch to feeding their cows silage which is a horrid muck
of molasses and grains and, believe it or not, sheep and cow
bits! It just doesn't seem natural. But the worst thing is it is
seeping into wonderful rivers like the Torridge and Taw and
the runs of salmon and trout are plummeting and nobody is
willing to do anything about it." As he pauses, the thrum-
ming of the jet engines seems to rise to a crescendo and then

fade as, with a wave of his now empty glass, he resumes: "In the sea, salmon farms, especially in Ireland, are potentiating sea lice so that they are finding smolts dead, completely covered in lice. And when any sea trout or salmon do survive to return as adults there are a few hundred gillnetters in the North Sea who refuse to lift their nets, demanding their historical rights to destroy the remains of the runs. And no one is willing to challenge them. The fisheries people have never disallowed a commercial fishery in favour of conservation. Can you believe the idiocy! I think I am ready to move to Alaska or B.C., where you have environmental protection and the Department of Fisheries actually manages for protection of fish stocks. Short of that, if it were up to me alone, I would give all my money to Greenpeace."

It is the longest speech I have ever heard him make. For a few long minutes, we sit in *folie-à-deux* silence, fuming at the human race's suicidal insanity, but eventually we soothe our inflamed nerves with more sips of single malt. He, wordlessly apoplectic, and I, with a sinking feeling of being the bearer of bad tidings, not wishing to disabuse him of his rosy vision of paradise in British Columbia by revealing to him the true state of things.

When I came to British Columbia, my first overwhelming impression was that I was now living in an immensely favoured part of the world. You can live in New York, London or Toronto for years and not take note of the natural environment, especially of wilderness, but in Vancouver you have to pay your dues to inhabit this extraordinarily privileged perch on the Pacific. In 1976, motivated to earn my place and, having stumbled upon the Steelhead Society of British Columbia, I felt I should throw my lot in with those who were so passionate about wild rivers and wild fish—as topics, less sexy than whales and giant trees, but integral to the health of the province's environment and in need of custodial attention, in fact, stewardship from people in the know, devoted anglers. And anglers pursuing the rarest, most beautiful, most difficult to catch and powerful freshwater fish of them all, the steelhead, were by definition most sensitive to the impending great loss represented by their declining numbers—in the dozens to hundreds and, occasionally, few thousands.

Genetically, steelhead are actually most closely related to Pacific salmon rather than to "true" brown trout *(Salmo trutta)*, although they don't die upon spawning. My own theory, informed by others, is that the original Polar salmon split into two groups, the Atlantic salmon *(Salmo salar)* and the Pacific salmon *(Oncorhynchus)*, and that the steelhead *(O. mykiss)*, the ancient, most primitive and so least specialized salmon, populated every ecological niche available from trickly creeks to giant rivers, working its way south from the pole all the way down to Baja California. The West Coast, having so many favourable ecological variations, produced increasingly specialized species, including chinook, coho, chum, pink and sockeye.

The Steelhead Society comprised wonderful people—
mostly men, some women—across the political spectrum
who devoted much time and effort to protecting the resource
through attending public meetings and writing countless
letters. It was largely a good old boys' organization fortunate to have attracted an unprecedented degree of dedica-
tion from its members, then headed by Cal Woods, a gentle,
kind and soft-spoken retired florist who was tough as nails
and worked full time as a volunteer. Combined with Eugene
Rogers, a hotter-tempered, more volatile but equally devoted
conservationist (and semi-retired real estate appraiser) and
Peter Broomhall, an indefatigable letter writer and college
instructor of English, as well as several others, the society
achieved some notable victories.

It fought against full-scale dredging of the Chilliwack-
Vedder River as a solution for major flooding of private
land that had occurred during spring freshets. Although the
public screamed about the required expropriation of land,
the berms created to let the river meander naturally remain
the main recreational thoroughfares for hikers, walkers,
bikers and horse riders, as well as anglers. Working with
other groups, the society managed to save a major portion
of the Squamish estuary from industrialization. And, most
importantly, when Carolin Mines polluted the Coquihalla
River through construction of a faulty cyanide-laced tailings
dam, the society led the way in the prosecution and lawsuit.

Having served as a director for twelve years, by 1988

I had an emerging vision for the society that was inspired when Cal, near death, took me aside and pointed out the organization had to become more professional, aggressive and self-sustaining.

"But you can't push people into things, Ehor," he cautioned. "These are good guys, but a lot more conservative than when I was a young militant." At my raised eyebrows, he went on to tell me of his more radical days during the Dirty Thirties. I loved it!

"You've got to make your points and lead and, if you are good at it and make sense, they will follow naturally."

The society needed a paid executive director and, additionally, prominent members of society with political clout and public profile who were also ardent conservationists and anglers. My first step had been to bring Ken Kirkby to a directors' meeting. He was both impressed and dismayed: "My God, you are trying to be everything to everyone! Is that possible or even wise?" But he was hooked and would go on to create numerous limited editions of prints that we at first gave away, then sold and eventually auctioned at our fundraisers towards my third goal: building a war chest to fight the good fight.

My next goal was to recruit at least one member of Vancouver society whose status and credentials no one could question and who could open any door, regardless of the wealth of the occupant or the hue of the politician therein. My opportunity arose when the Haig-Brown Flyfishers asked me to make the feature presentation at their Christmas banquet. Among the guests of honour was Henry "Budge" Bell-Irving, the lieutenant-governor of British Columbia. Budge was from one of British Columbia's oldest families, one that had owned a large commercial salmon fishing and canning company. In addition, he was a highly decorated war hero, having risen to brigadier and led Canadian troops into Amsterdam during its liberation. After my presentation, Budge said: "Young man, when I am finished with this job I am going to look you up, we are going to go fishing, you are going to tell me about the Steelhead Society and I am going to introduce you to a few people." I was elated. Budge would become an integral part of my plan, a powerful ally and a close friend. It was clear that I had been given a rare opportunity to combine connections with the corporate, political and royalist sensibilities of British Columbia, putting them to the service of conservation. And if I waited for my moment, river conservationists in British Columbia could acquire in Ted yet another powerful ally.

Glancing out of the airplane window at the beds of clouds below, I search for a happier topic. I tell Ted of the wonderful fishing I had on the Squamish River and on the Thompson and how Alexei even grabbed a small rod and waved it about as he waded into the shallows. Ted's face transforms into a map of myriad smile lines. Fishing and children, it is clear, are the antidote to Ted's gloomy moments, rare as they are. Or perhaps, as I ponder the violence in his poetry—the skull-crushing assault in "Law in the Country of the Cats," the pitiless eponymous "Crow Tyrannosaurus" and the fatal choice made in "The Gatekeeper"—not so rare.

After retrieving my four-wheel drive we head for the new digs on Pasco Road. As we tilt down that goat trail just outside Horseshoe Bay, the great trees form a bower of lush green through which the ocean occasionally glints cerulean blue. Ted blurts out: "My God, Ehor. This is amazing. You haven't lost Deep Cove; you've traded it for another paradise. How can something like this exist so close to the city?"

After my travels, the uninterrupted beauty is a balm. Only twenty minutes from downtown, eagles haunt the giant cedars with their frail cries, seals compete with them for fish, and cougars and bears are frequently seen stalking through the old-growth forest that somehow escaped the logger's saw a hundred years ago. This is home and worth fighting for.

I unlock the door, and we enter a construction site that seems to have even fewer amenities than when I left some weeks before. This is hardly what the contractor promised. Nothing is ready, no kitchen, not even the toilets or faucets work. I am about to say that we can't stay here when I hear snoring: Ted is on the bare plywood floor, fast asleep. I'm expecting Vicky and Alexei back the next day and wondering what to do when the phone rings. It is my friend Rob Mingay.

"How was the trip? When did you get back?"

"Two minutes ago," I answer wearily and start to describe my predicament.

"Wait!" says Rob, who explains he's leaving for three weeks and wants to return our cat first. "Do you guys want to stay here while I am away?"

Perhaps there is a God, I ponder through a veil of exhaustion. How reality can change in a few words! How good it is to have friends! I rouse Ted from his instantaneous hibernation and, a little bemused, he plods behind me carrying his bags of gear back to the truck. We arrive at Rob's place thirty minutes later, soaked in the sweat of summer heat and fatigue. Within half an hour we are showered and drinking duty-free single malts; in an hour we are tucked into our beds, gifts from kind providence and Rob's big heart, and dreaming of steelhead slashing at our flies.

At the airport the next day, Alexei is wearing a blissful smile and clinging to me like I'm a lifeline. Ted comments that children, like animals, need to reimprint on their parents or closest members of the pack after long separations. My friend Jay Rowland appears with Ron Cordes in tow. After greetings all around, Jay decrees in his nasal tones that he is tired of being responsible for every meal, so henceforth everyone has to prepare at least one or two. Ted does a double take, then allows: "I used to cook when I had the children on my own, but lately, Jay, I've been infantilized. I have a wife who is a splendid cook and, for the past two decades, I've done nothing more than make tea. I am afraid I may be a bit useless on that count."

"Well, prepare something ahead of time, Ted. I want everyone to pitch in. I'm sure Vicky will help you out."

"Of course I'll help," she chimes in.

"I suppose I could manage spaghetti," Ted hazards.

It becomes the great culinary campaign: Ted's shopping for ingredients, including special Italian wines and spices, culminates in a major kitchen onslaught that enlists the use of innumerable pots, pans and utensils, permeating the environs with a rich mélange of tangy aromas as we swill wine and observe reluctant chef Ted. Miraculously, after several hours, he pours out several huge jars full of wonderful, thick red sauce from the great vat on the stove and, having worked himself into a lather that would shame a racehorse, declares the war won. Enough spaghetti sauce and garlic bread to feed an army lie arranged on the kitchen table.

.   .   .

ONCE AGAIN THE flight to the Dean is bathed in August sunlight, but this time Ted is more animated: pointing out rivers, wondering what they hold, commenting on especially impressive peaks like Mount Waddington—at well over thirteen thousand feet the coastal range's tallest and most dramatic massif with a peak that slices swordlike into the sky. I describe to Ted how two Canadians, Don and Phyllis Munday, spotted it on a climbing trip on Vancouver Island in the 1920s and presumed it was British Columbia's tallest, dubbing it Mystery Mountain.

"I can't get over how young this land is," he says softly. "It is like getting to know a child, a magnificent, mysterious and somewhat intimidating child."

From our height above the Chilcotin plateau, I point out the road planned in the 1800s by entrepreneurs who intended a major settlement there but did not ask the aboriginals' permission to cross their land and so incurred the wrath of the Tsilqot'in. The ensuing massacre of the road-building crew and subsequent hunting-down and hanging of five native men involved in the uprising, despite the Tsilqot'in's agreement to negotiate, is one of the few episodes of mass violence in B.C. history. In one sense, the aboriginal people did win: the area remained practically untouched, even by widespread logging, until the late 1970s. In an ironic way, we are benefiting from that conflict, for had the road gone through, the Dean would almost certainly not have retained its pure wilderness state. Benefiting as well are the herds of wild horses that inhabit the Nemiah Valley, the largest numbers left in British Columbia, allegedly direct descendants of those brought over by the conquistadors. Ted comments that horses originated in North America but that ironically, local tribes rather than domesticating them wiped them out so that only a few survivors made their way across the land bridge to Asia and Europe, where the inhabitants more wisely captured them and turned them into transportation, triggering a revolution in ground travel. Demonstrating the power of ideas, this time the locals got it. It is as close to real cowboy country as still exists anywhere in North America, and a hunter and fisherman's Valhalla.

And once again we are greeted by Lee and his outgoing crew, who have hooked twenty-six steelhead and landed fifteen. The number landed is of greater consequence, whether for food if the angler is in the habit of killing fish or for bragging rights if he releases them. On the Dean, fishing is about catch-and-release, not gathering protein. As Martin Tolley, a founding member of the Totem Flyfishers, once said, "A steelhead is too valuable to be caught only once."

"The nicest thing about the second trip," Ted comments, "is that one has the memory of the first to enhance the anticipation and lace it with the sounds and smells and feel of the place." Anticipation is quickly cut short. Within an hour the four of us are hiking down the river in our waders, breathing in the sinus-clearing fragrance of the great cedars and pausing to look at the structure of the Jam Hole, the initial refuge for steelhead that have overcome the daunting chutes and torrents of the first falls five kilometres from the sea. "This is a pool that honour decrees you should fish with a dry fly, Ted," I pronounce.

"Honour, Ehor?" Ted regards me bemusedly.

"These fish have struggled so hard to make it up this incredible falls that you should tempt only those with the strength and audacity to rise to the surface to attack a fly. Darwin's natural selection suggests they will be especially worthy specimens."

Ted and I return to a topic of frequent consideration: the special pleasures of dry-fly fishing, which involves using a fly that floats rather than sinks, so that the fish must rise to take it, making for a very dramatic appearance on the surface. It is the most sensuous, gratifying and difficult way to hook a steelhead. A kind of rapture overtakes you when that fly disappears in the vortex of the swirls of a mighty fish, for when a big fish takes the fly it is often a much slower process than that of the rising trout. The most important thing is not to strike, for that would pull the fly out of the fish's mouth before it is hooked, but rather to wait during those eternal split seconds until the fish turns and in descent pulls down your rod. Then she is yours.

"I've thought a lot about what you have said . . . about the multidimensional pleasures of dry-fly fishing," Ted says, "and I've written a poem about it. I have yet to hook a salmon or steelhead on the dry but perhaps this trip . . ." Despite, my pleas, Ted declines to recite the poem, merely paraphrasing it, begging imperfect memory, but I track it down later. It is titled "Be a Dry-Fly Purist":

> Barely prick the meniscus. Lightly caress
> The last gleam on the river. Lift off deftly
> As a sedge-fly. Keep your head clear
> Keep your body keep your soul clear
> Of the river-fetch . . .

"There he is!" Ted shouts as the mate to his steelhead of the previous year cartwheels over the pool. After a struggle that belies its modest size, Ted lands the eight-pounder on the far side. Jay rolls one twice, I have one mighty pull on a Sustut River Snake fly and Ron caps it off with a lively opener that leaps eight times. And then, as happens so many times, the fresh pod moves upstream and the river goes dead.

The brilliant late-summer sun has dimmed to burnished bronze as we drag ourselves back to camp. We slump into our suddenly luxurious camp chairs. I pull off the cloying waders, clammy light woollen shirt and fleece, and plunge into a back eddy pool at the foot of the cutbank. "Aiee!" I come barrelling out of the water with a blood-curdling scream, having forgotten that the river is only fifty-five degrees Fahrenheit. I am definitely reinvigorated. The others chuckle and settle for freshening up with a few splashes of water on their faces. My teeth chattering, I bustle around in the underbrush in a pair of dry long johns, gathering kindling as Jay fires up the camp stove. Changed into fresh clothes, we arrange ourselves around the blazing fire on our spindly aluminum chairs and sip some of the first B.C. Sauvignon Blanc worth writing home about. We dine on seafood paella, loaded with crab, shrimp, prawns, scallops and clams. Sinful cinnamon cake and Monte Cristo coffees topped with whipped cream put a lisp into our postsupper conversations and we fall into bed.

Dawn brings rain and wind, but we are on the water by half past seven with no competition in sight, a relief since the only real anxiety on the Dean, despite its remoteness, is the number of other anglers with whom you have to share a pool. The benign mountain-ringed landscape of the previous evening is reduced to low scudding clouds and sheets of icy rain and wind that almost manage to penetrate our layers of underwear, cotton shirts, woollen sweaters, nylon chest waders and hooded rain slickers. Even as Ted and I walk down to the Victoria Run, Jay's yahoos announce he is into a fine fish—a sixteen-pounder—right in front of the camp. Ted and I start fishing and Ted can do no wrong: within an hour he has hooked three, landed two, all slightly above the twelve-pound Dean average. The fish, as always, are almost diaphanous in their chrome splendour, glowing "grey or silver ghosts" some people call them, each deserving a protracted reflection on their beauty as they slowly come back to life and, with an insolent flick of their tails, free themselves from our grasp and vanish into the aquamarine currents. Sometimes I am almost overcome with an urge to follow. Not for some melodramatically tragic reason; it just seems fitting, in this setting of softly hissing currents, sweepers of fallen Douglas firs gently undulating in the current and waves breaking over the rocks, to provide perfect lies for these perfect creatures that we never tire of pursuing.

Ted refuses to continue until I hook my first, gently suggesting I emulate his methods. I have now gone through the run twice with a dry fly. Swallowing my preference and my pride, I put away my floating line and dry fly and, following Ted's example, loop on a high-speed, high-density sinking tip to the end of my floating fly line to which I affix a Davie Street Hooker. Now my fly will probe the depths where the steelhead lie rather than trying to lure them to the surface.

On the third lengthening cast, my line tightens at forty-five degrees downstream and I am into a heavy fish that runs at me, thank God, but even as my line is still upstream it bolts towards the sea and, unfortunately, the logjam I have been dreading. I bound over the sweepers at water's edge and manage to get it downstream of the morass of logs, where it dogs in the tailout of the pool, and I force it to shore: a very heavy-bodied supernally radiant female panting in the shallows, eighteen to twenty pounds.

I comment to Ted that even after having caught so many, this glistening, silver wraith still takes my breath away in the same way that a beautiful woman doffing her clothes continues to do.

"Good thing you don't have to choose!" Ted shouts in congratulation as I watch the steelhead amble away into the depths, wearing the defiant sneer of a fresh-run doe. I cast again and very quickly I am into another, more dogged, beast, perhaps a buck that, alas, wraps itself around a sweeper. As I pull to free myself, my line slingshots back at me without my only high-speed sink tip. Perhaps the revenge of my first fish's jealous suitor? I could be in trouble if the water turns deep and dirty and floating lines become ineffectual.

That night we are awakened by torrential rains accompanied by gale-force winds that threaten to lift off the tarpaulin cowling and tent. Roused from their beds by the storm's howling and now soaked to the skin, Ron and Ted hold on to the traces as if their lives depend on it. Jay and I scuttle about grabbing short logs to lash them to, then pile them high with rocks as big as we can carry. An hour later, the tent secure, we towel ourselves down and crawl back into our beds. The storm rampages unabated.

At eleven the next morning we rise and cook an elaborate breakfast, watching other anglers pound the murky waters opposite. We experience the ambivalence that accompanies the spectacle of the competition fishing: we want them to catch fish to show it can be done, but not so many that we feel bad for not being out there ourselves. They catch none and we return to drinking coffee, tying flies, telling stories and reading. Ted starts to write, but at Jay's behest gives it up to fashion a table for us using a chainsaw. Even for a laureate, the survival hierarchy of the wilderness camp, dictated by the camp commissar, demands practical production over pure art. I wonder if this is an efficient use of the poet's time, but an hour later we stand around admiring a piece of furniture that is quite sturdy and serviceable. I silently chastise myself for doubting the outcome. The verse can wait.

We spend a lazy day watching the water. Suddenly Jay spots splashing and swirling in the tail of the camp pool and sounds the alarm. Within minutes, he and Ron are dressed and across the river in the little raft. Ted and I head down to Victoria. Jay hooks fish after fish, mostly behind Ron, then Ron starts to get takes. Ted and I flog the water impotently, only slightly soothed by the never mundane phenomenon of lovely, fragile pale evening duns, mayflies, rising from the river's surface, occasionally being taken by what we presume are cutthroat, so delicate is their sipping. Oh, for a trout rod, we lament! Jay returns to camp having landed three of four hooked; Ron, three of three. Ted and I, fishless, bravely congratulate our camp mates.

The next day breaks cool and clear. The magnificent line of mountain peaks to the north glows under a cloak of fresh snow, and our spirits soar. This time Ron and Jay hustle down to Victoria, with Jay rowing over in a rapidly deflating raft. Not cautious Jay's idea of an idyllic crossing, but he makes it. Almost immediately he hooks a fish of such proportions that everyone but Ron stops to watch. It tears up and down the river and then decides after fifteen minutes to return to the sea, at least ten kilometres below us. We watch Jay chase it a kilometre downstream into the fabled and perilous Stump Pool. A half hour later a dejected Jay reappears with a tale of playing the fish for twenty-five minutes but, just as it was tiring, it wrapped itself around a stump and broke off.

Finally I feel the comforting weight of a heavy take on my deep-sunk fly. It explodes on the surface before motoring downstream. I look down to see my reel literally smoking and shrieking. I am now in Victoria opposite Ron, who actually stops casting for a nanosecond to cheer me on as I continue my chase another hundred metres, but then I spot a logjam below with a giant sweeper perfectly situated to snag my line. There is only one thing to do: put on the brakes and pray. I clamp down and the fish begins to turn; my rod is bent double and my wrist burns with exhaustion. I begin to wind and, yes! The mighty fish is coming in. Ever so slowly I continue winding as smoothly as possible, not wanting to inspire any more panic-stricken runs. Almost ten minutes later my shooting head reappears, but the water is too murky to spot the fish. He is almost in but won't come any farther and starts to shake his head, a very bad sign. And the leader—chafed on the rocks, his jaw and, God forbid, perhaps a wind knot—parts. I slump onto the cobbles, exhausted physically and emotionally. Steelhead one, Ehor zero. And on a banner day, when Ron lands six of seven, Jay four of six and, thank heaven, Ted three of three, it is the only fish I encounter.

My companions, in the throes of their celebrations, offer words of sympathy. In their gentle way, they are underscoring the fact that I am the goat and I hate it but laugh it off. The steaks and the delicious Australian Shiraz that night help a great deal. And Ted makes it his mission to cheer me up. Taking over as raconteur he enthralls us with a story of pike fishing with Nick on a lough in Ireland, where they were gently interrogated in a bar by the locals, and then the next day they snagged a heavy object deep in the lake that they started to raise by its rope until they realized just when it came into sight they were being watched through binoculars from shore: it was a heavy burlap bag. They quickly let it sink, hightailed it to shore and sped away in their car to another lough, presumably almost having become entangled with the IRA.

My dreams are haunted by that giant fish. What fragile creatures we mortals be, our self-worth dependent on the mere landing of a fish, a creature totally oblivious to our existence. We awaken filled with boundless optimism, the world crackling with negative ions and an intense freshness that injects energy straight into the veins: the first portent of autumn, my favourite time. Gold cottonwood leaves the size of doubloons rattle in the trees above the riverbank. Today is the last day we have the lower river to ourselves. Tomorrow is the first of September, when the jet boats of the guides are allowed to descend this far.

We pass around bowls of cereal and cups of coffee even while donning our waders, then head for the river. Ted and I walk to Victoria as clouds of pale evening duns hover like golden fairy helicopters over the river. We cross back channels of the river, where Ted is thrilled to spot thousands of fry happily living and growing until they are of a size to smolt and head downstream. The world feels, looks and smells fecund and healthy today. Even though we are anxious to wet a line, we pause to drink in the richness of the scene. "Being here adds years to one's life," Ted says softly. "Remind me of that, Ehor, if I ever get too caught up in the morass of my overcommitted life sentence and pass up your invitation in future. It is tough to get away when everyone wants a piece of you."

I step into the river and immediately have a take. I land it, a sea-lice-free fifteen-pounder, without much ado—not

challenging, but after yesterday's zero, mightily reassuring.
I bid him thanks for restoring my fragile sense of self-worth
even as I say adieu. And then I watch as Ted puts on a show
worthy of the palace guard: within an hour he has hooked
four, landed three, the biggest a mate for mine, in the neck of
Victoria. We start hitting fish regularly throughout the day,
with Jay repeating my battle with a giant almost as if scripted,
ending with his choosing to break him off as he headed for
the same sweeper that cost me my flyline two days ago. On
the other side, Ron, never one to betray much excitement,
almost verbalizes as he battles a mighty fish that, given
the lack of obstacles, he lands within ten minutes: a thirty-
nine-inch beauty. He lands four more in four more passes. It
occurs to all of us that something very special is happening:
a pod of mighty fish is moving upstream and we are here all
alone to intercept it.

When the smoke clears, I have landed four, two more
than twenty pounds. By now everyone is repairing to camp
to prepare the midday meal, but I manage to turn Ted and
convince him to take my place in the run. Within a couple of
casts he is into a ferocious silvery wraith that crashes about
the pool and takes off downstream, but Ted's mighty Bruce
and Walker eventually turns her and brings her still battling
to the beach: his biggest ever. We know more great fish are
passing us, but we are exhausted and, luxuriating in the joy
of wasting great fishing, we choose to walk back savouring
an extraordinary morning.

In the evening, I cross Victoria and hook what I think is a frail pink salmon that I lead towards me until I try to derrick it unceremoniously to shore and suddenly all hell breaks loose. Before I know it, my prize has sped into the flow and below the logjam, forcing me once again to dipsy-doodle among the logs and dip my rod underwater and around the sweeper. I am almost bemused when fifteen minutes later I am able to beach it: a great slab of a buck that measures out at twenty by thirty-nine inches and, as I have come prepared with a cotton twine net basket and scale, twenty-three pounds by weight, my third biggest.

A giant race of fish has come up the river today, and everyone has hooked at least one more than twenty pounds. It is my best Dean River day ever.

We are all laughing and sipping wine around the fire waiting for what I dub rather cornily TLS (Ted's Legendary Spaghetti, or The Laureate Spaghetti; an allusion to the *Times Literary Supplement*), when Ron, upon reading the day's log, begins to splutter: "What, you couldn't have hooked seven, Ehor!"

"Why not, Ron?"

"I never saw you hook that many in any day, including today."

"But *I* did," says Ted. "What seems to be the matter?"

"He couldn't have landed them all," insists Ron.

"Well, I did, Ron," I retort.

Ron, who somehow manages to lose very few, shrugs as

the rest of us chuckle. The spaghetti is superb and we end up
feeding the hungry passing masses. Not fishes and loaves but
every bit as appreciated.

Reveille is very early the next morning, and so we are
all in position on the pool as the hateful whine of jet boats
shatters the serenity of the postdawn. The guides drop off
their clients down the length of the pool and then jet up and
down checking on them, irritating us. Nevertheless, we have
a banner day. That night as I take a turn writing down the
log I ask Ron: "How many?"

"Six for eight," he offers, his nose in a science-fiction
novel.

"How many witnessed?" asks Ted. Ron does not answer.

We vacate the campfire at eleven in order to take on the
jet boats the next morning. The lackadaisical tenor of the trip
has changed.

We rise at half past five, slurping cereal to be on the run
before the sun—and the hounds from hell, who in actu-
ality are very nice people, as are the young men guiding
them. Jay goes through Victoria and, like clockwork as he
passes opposite the fabled logjam, hooks a lovely acrobatic
steelhead. Ron follows and gets nothing. I come behind him
and—slam—am instantly into a fish that I point out to him
as I land: retribution! A beautiful eighteen-pounder that Ron
graciously acknowledges. As we prepare to come in under
the blazing noonday sun, we note the water is turning milky,
a sure sign that the glacier is melting.

Waiting for us at camp are my dear friend John Hamill and three other anglers. We take no more fish that day, but that night we feast on a magnificent filet that John prepares along with poetic spaghetti, salad, mussels, smoked salmon and fine Pinot Gris. Sitting around the campfire after, we share a bottle of Brad Bennett's generously proffered Courvoisier that fuels more stories, until the Milky Way is shimmering overhead and the northern lights start to pass over us in crackling green waves. Another trip for the ages.

Upon returning to Vancouver, we are met at the airport by Lee Straight, come to find out how the camp had stood up, given word that had filtered south of ferocious storms driving several camping parties off the river. Scanning the Totem trip log for our week—eighty-three hooked, sixty-seven landed—Lee clucks skeptically: "Do you fellows always hook more than eighty fish even when battling high water?"

"We should have caught more," I retort. "After all, we lost almost a day fishing and I kept trying to raise them on the dry."

"I look forward to the photos. Got to have photos, as I always say," Lee chuckles as he waves goodbye.

As Vicky pulls up to take us home, Ted offers: "Any bets that Vicky has built a fire under those contractors?"

"That would be amazing," I say, and so it is. Our new house, still in a rough state, is now fully occupied. We dub it Alba, after the Roman name for Scotland. That order of business resolved, I turn my attention to politics. My first priority is to put Budge Bell-Irving together with Ted and try to come up with a plan to promote conservation using their combined attributes and connections. Budge arrives at Pasco Road wearing a sports coat, so I know he hasn't quite sussed out what sort of occasion this is supposed to be. In fact, it is a little awkward initially, as it is clear Budge is more familiar than Ted with the royal family and the attendant pomp and circumstance, and he does not know what to make of this quiet, hulking Yorkshire poet.

The conversation is pleasant enough but rather constrained, with Budge retreating into his slightly officious and safe, but friendly, lieutenant-governor style and Ted becoming somewhat guarded. Ted, ever honest, has to admit to Budge's innocent inquiries that he has met the queen only once or twice and so is obviously not an insider. I realize I am talking too much to fill the awkward gaps. Finally, I inject the element that always works with a certain type.

"Ted and I just got back from the Dean, Budge."

"Did you! Isn't that an amazing river? I have never had better fishing and caught more powerful fish. Did you have good fishing?"

"The best," jumps in Ted, "and my biggest steelhead ever."

"How big . . . ?" And I sit back and watch two anglers wax rhapsodic over a common passion. After a half hour of trading anecdotes, Budge asks: "Do you ever fish for salmon back home?"

"Oh, yes, we have a nice stretch on the Exe in Devon, but my most enjoyable time has been fishing the queen mother's water in Scotland and, even better, sharing evenings with her just chatting and sipping Scotch."

That is obviously the clincher: Budge, like everyone, adores the queen mother.

"Isn't she a delight? And such a gracious hostess. Was Charles there?" Budge beams.

"No, though I have been her guest a couple of times. But she appears to love him dearly."

"Yes, she is quite worried about him, I imagine." By the end Budge is proclaiming they must do something together in aid of B.C. steelhead.

Before Ted leaves, Ken arrives from Toronto with great stories of his latest conquests. They are in part political, having met the premier of Ontario and the Speaker of the House of Commons. A second victory is his sale of large paintings to prominent Toronto businessmen. And third, his plan to paint the largest painting ever on canvas: a panorama of the Arctic landscape.

Sitting around one evening, sharing a bottle of Glenmorangie, I hear the longed-for words from Ted: "Perhaps, Ken, we can combine to do something that could raise a little money for the Steelhead Society? You do a river picture, I scribble some lines, say about the Dean River, and we flog it at a fundraiser."

"I love it," says Ken, ever the enthusiastic supporter.

"Send me some verse and I will choose an image." We talk late into the night, describing the Dean River to Ken, who has never been there but nevertheless believes in the steelhead as an important symbol of survival of the wilderness. "I've got to make a trip there sometime," he confirms. Suddenly the bottle is empty.

Ted writes on Christmas Day, 1988, that he is sending us the poem that he wishes us to use in any way we deem appropriate, and how he is thinking of us in our "great house of light" in the "wheelhouse" of the Pacific with the surf crashing on the rocks under our bowsprit.

Ken loves the poem, which is "The Bear," and with Ted's permission for us to use it as we wish, we choose a portion to go with a brooding drawing that Ken makes of the Victoria Run where we and many others have had extraordinary experiences. It is a big hit offered as a bonus to attendees at the Steelhead Society banquet. A major success for our first foray.

5 / A HOUSE DIVIDED

It is an intense year. The house the contractor predicted would be completed when we returned from Europe in August is not ready until the following July. We live with various contractors and tradespeople for nine months, including a superb welder, a Popeye-like Hell's Angel named Dale Wickert who does a masterful job of the ironwork on the deck and gate. When he comes in for coffee each morning he proves the best at motivating the infant Alexei: "Eat your yogurt, kid," he growls, and a properly impressed Alexei complies, wide-eyed. We offer Dale a job as a nanny but, unsurprisingly, he turns us down.

When it's finally done, Alba, with its remote wilderness atmosphere despite its proximity to downtown Vancouver, is well worth the wait.

ON A SUN-DRENCHED August afternoon in 1989 our
Hughes helicopter throbs past glaciers and mountain goats,
cascading waterfalls and the complex, intact estuary of the
Dean, an unusual natural state in this age of dredged, chan-
nellized and industrialized river mouths. There are neither
piers nor dikes nor retaining walls where the fresh, glacially
tinted, shifting waters of the Dean meet the sea. Even from
the chopper we can see salmon swirling along the beach: an
odd phenomenon, chum actually spawning in the sea thanks
to upwelling fresh water along the strand. We land to be
greeted by a group of Osprey Flyfishers' club members who
have had a good trip, landing thirty of fifty-five hooked.

It is hot, perhaps ninety degrees Fahrenheit, and so we
wear only fishing shirts of cotton or perforated nylon and
long johns under our waders. Ted's waders are made of skin
divers' neoprene and he sweats profusely as we make our
way to the river. Mine are thin nylon so they have no insulating quality but are better for hiking in the bake-oven heat
of the valley and besides, my first reading reveals the water
temperature is fifty-nine degrees, not terribly cold and ideal
for persuading a steelhead to rise to a dry fly.

That first afternoon, however, we get nothing, though a
new outfitter organizing tours of foreign anglers reports several hooked before us in Victoria. That evening as the shadows lengthen and the sun moves off the water we cross the
Camp Run. It is still pleasantly warm as I tie on a Thompson

River Rat, a spun white caribou hair dry (floating) fly the shape of a football with a green polar bear wing and tail. I see fish rolling on the surface in the shallow tailout of the pool, so I gradually lengthen the amount of line with succeeding casts until I am carrying about eighty feet on my presentation. As the fly sputters past, a rising bulge stretches the surface and the fly disappears. I withstand the urge to strike—that would only pull the fly away from the fish—and instead drop my rod tip and release the eighteen-inch loop of line in my free hand. It works. The slack allows the fish to ingest the fly and it turns and clamps down. Seconds later, I lift my rod slightly and the fish goes berserk, exploding fully three feet into the air, a silver crescent of hammered steel. Within an hour I land two of three aggressive fish but am a little chagrined that, over the course of the day, Ted loses his only fish on an express train–like run down river.

To top it off, Ted has been made exempt from culinary duties and is now the chief dishwasher. We have had our traditionally splendid inaugural seafood dinner: fresh prawns and scallops marinated in garlic and ginger with basmati rice, accompanied by Greek salad and toasted garlic bread and followed by coffee with Baileys and Häagen-Dazs ice cream slathered with chocolate sauce. The fire over which we try to cook most of our meals has been stoked to a roaring blaze, so we are leaning back in our chairs staring into it while Ted, wearing a rather fetching blue floral apron that some wag has brought along, is up to his elbows in dishwater.

Unlike Ted, Jay has had a productive day on the river and revels in the poetic justice of the scene. "Tell me, Ted," he ventures. "Is there any chance, being the Poet Laureate, that you'll be knighted?"

"Very likely, Jay, though I'm not sure I would accept," he responds among the clatter of pots and pans.

"What! Why would you ever turn it down?"

"Well, it's bad enough that being Poet Laureate means most other writers despise you. But being knighted would be the nail in the coffin. Total estrangement from the literary community and reality, not to mention my roots."

"But wouldn't your wife like it?"

"Of course she would, and that might be why I would accept."

"Well, I would advise you to accept, Ted. You would always be welcome to come back here and do the dishes for us as Sir Ted."

We all laugh, savouring the contrast between that image and the memory of Ted's most recent public poetry performance.

Only days before, Jay had held his fortieth birthday party at O'Doul's, a hotel restaurant and jazz bar in Vancouver. I told Ted that as a group gift we had bought Jay a lovely STH fly reel, appropriately inscribed. Ted was chagrined that he hadn't been able to contribute to it. "No problem, Ted. You can compose a poem to read out at dinner."

"How far away is this place?" he queried.

"Twenty minutes. You've got more than enough time, I'm sure, if you don't spare the scatological."

"Are you sure no one will be offended?"

"Of course not, Ted. This is a pretty rough crowd," I assured him, lying through my teeth and mischievously picturing at least two devout, sheltered Christians who might be taken aback.

"I'll do my best." Ted ripped a sheet out of his notebook and commenced what he always referred to as "scribbling."

The party, comprising a motley crew rounded up by Jay's brother Scott, was in full swing when we arrived. Some were Jay's boyhood friends; others, members of the Totems like Bob Taylor and Lee Straight, easily the oldest in the room; still others were Jay's friends from work and his social life away from fishing. O'Doul's is a "fern bar" where denizens of Vancouver's West End gather to drink and listen to jazz, but on this night we dominated one large corner. After drinks, a meal and the presentation of the reel, each of us contributed an anecdote to a gentle roasting of the guest of honour.

When it was Ted's turn, he explained he didn't know Jay as well as some of the others, but "spending two weeks so far in isolation with a man gives you some insight into his character which might be best summed up in verse." There was a hush in the room: the Poet Laureate was actually going to read a poem about their friend. And so Ted began in a sonorous voice that caught the attention of some very cute passersby, who stopped to listen. Demonstrating he was no prude, Ted characterized the poem as a charm to keep

Jay from harm and then recited a descending series of bawdy rhyming couplets that would make a hip-hop artist blush . . . and feel envy for its clever inventiveness.

Guffaws broke out throughout the group, save for the couple of fellows I had wagered might be mortified by the verse. "Somehow, I thought the Poet Laureate's birthday poem would have a different, more elevated tone, Ted," Jay said in his wry voice. "What does the royal family think of this type of work?"

"Well, I don't think I will include it in my forthcoming royal celebratory collection," retorted Ted. Seizing the opportunity of the moment of complete silence in the room, the cuties who had stopped to listen having vanished, I declared that should the Poet Laureate gig ever dry up, Ted could wear his trousers even lower, adopt basketball shoes as regular foot gear and eke out a living in Los Angeles as a rapper. Since the genre had yet to penetrate much of regular culture, much less the ethereal world of the Poet Laureate, my allusion was lost on Ted; I explained to him how rapping began in African-American ghettos as a form of defence against physical violence when rivals met on street corners. He who could produce more insulting rhyming couplets rather than resorting to violence, won. As Ted did with every kind of public versifying, he showed some interest but we never pursued the topic.

Back at camp, England's Poet Laureate, relegated now to the status of kitchen help, crosses over to the far side of the Camp Run with me the next morning before the sun has cleared the eastern mountain peaks. In contrast to the midday heat, the mornings are chilly and we wear our down vests and woolly sweaters tucked into our waders. But we are not the first to wet a line today. The campers, unguided independent anglers like us, have already killed two steelhead—either short of food or preparing to leave.

I cast my dry fly into the current and even as I track its path downstream there is a slashing rise that starts me from my reverie. I am soundly connected to a nice fish of about twelve pounds that puts up a startlingly determined tussle, taking out all my flyline and most of the backing line on my reel, forcing me to chase it downstream. Fish that take dry flies are among the most athletic and powerful of their kind, and in this case, she's beautifully proportioned and almost transparent in her ocean brightness. A near perfect steelhead experience. Upon beaching it I feel strangely fulfilled and decide to relinquish the run to Ted. What more could one ask from the river than what just happened?

It is Ted's good fortune. Every cast brings a pull or lunge at his deep-sunk fly. And I watch the carousel-like performance of his hooking fish, chasing them downstream, landing them and returning to his station to cast again. Fish after fish falls to his Squamish Poacher.

"Ehor," he implores, "take a turn! There is a flotilla of steelhead passing through."

"Naw. You paid your dues. It's your show." Sometimes there can be no greater pleasure than watching a friend take advantage of an orgiastic drama of excess. Ted will long remember the morning he hooked seven steelhead and felt the unbridled joy experienced by too few anglers in this world. Across the river six Nova Scotians cheer him on. Ted's biggest, a mighty buck, weighs in at nineteen-and-a-half pounds. Ted is relishing his extraordinary luck with all the ingenuous pleasure a shy, fantasy-ridden schoolboy might show at being attacked by a bevy of beautiful older girls on the bus ride home. His face glowing, he says quietly: "I don't know why you did it, but thank you, Ehor."

The next day and a half is very slow. Nevertheless the afterglow carries Ted into the second evening's campfire and, at Jay's prompting, he waxes loquacious with ghost story after ghost story. The last is the most chilling.

"What about groups of ghosts?" asks a wide-eyed Jay, relishing the chills running down his spine. "Are ghosts ever seen in gangs?"

"Oh, yes," says Ted, staring off with heavy-lidded eyes towards the vertical cliffs behind our camp. The rising moon bathes them in an eerie white light. Ted pauses dramatically and sips his Scotch. "Two come to mind. One is a whole Roman legion that is often seen on certain nights in Devon, marching across the horizon. Some even say they hear the drumbeats. The most horrific is about a mill town where a lot of poor country boys came to get employment in the wool mill. They were hard workers but the owner became frustrated because they would sneak back home at night for harvest time or if they had accumulated enough money to pay off a debt. And it was a time of robber barons when the boss was king, prior to unions or government regulations. One night, when he had a crucial order to fill and his manager told him that several lads were planning to fly the coop that night, the owner had them locked in the mill where they were bunking. Sometime that night a terrible fire broke out, and the men couldn't get out. By the time the townspeople got to the mill, it was an inferno and the night air was filled with the agonized screams of men burning to death."

"What happened after?" asks the usually taciturn Ron, getting into the spirit of the moment.

"At least once a month the town was haunted by men in flames, fleeing and screaming as they made their way to the owner's mansion."

Jay shoots up out of his chair yelping in surprise: a cheeky mouse crawled up his pant leg at precisely the climactic moment. He traps the culprit in his pants with a hand over the cloth and, undoing them, releases his captive, which scurries away, none the worse for wear—literally. Then Jay looks up towards the north.

"My God, look at that." A crackling, hissing, green wave of aurora borealis is heading right at us, seemingly at tree-top height. It explodes overhead in a space-bound whirlpool of pink and green icy flame. We have had some fine displays of northern lights on our trips, but nothing like this. The heavenly barrage of eerie dancing light and low, almost subliminal buzzing goes on for more than half an hour, then stampedes towards the north, a herd of bounding, gazellelike poltergeists. We climb into our sleeping bags in silence. In the distance a wolf howls, its cry rebounding along the cliff faces of the valley.

In the last two days, I hook eight fish and, even though our hooked and landed totals are down slightly, the trip has been a great success. Each one of us has had at least one day of several fish hooked and landed. And for once someone other than Ron, our Eveready fishing machine, is top rod. Ted has encountered the most fish but neither he nor Ron seems to pay it much attention.

On that last evening Jay grills a ten-pounder that bled upon being landed, a rare occurrence, and we feed the Nova Scotia crew, who turn out to be great company. I lived on the South Shore, on St. Margaret's Bay, while teaching at Dalhousie University in Halifax and learned to fly-fish for salmon on the Atlantic salmon streams of the mainland and Cape Breton. We trade stories of Nova Scotia, my second-favourite place in the world. Ted, as usual, plies them for information about the salmon fishing but they lament the downward plunge of stocks, a phenomenon also plaguing Europe.

Ted is in fine fettle and clearly in a storytelling mood. So Jay asks him how he met his present wife.

"I was taking care of both children and my aged, ailing parents back at Court Green in Devon and wasn't sure how I would cope. I had even thought of taking a job when *deus ex machina* struck: I won a German poetry fellowship that I hadn't even applied for. Apparently a school teacher up north had for some reason put forth my name, God bless her. But I still needed someone to help me with the children and my parents so that I could write. One day I was out eel fishing with a local lad named Orchard when I happened to mention to him my situation. Well, he said he had a teenaged sister who had just completed nurse's training and was looking for a position locally. It was Carol and she was a godsend. Both children took to her right away, and within months my mother took me aside and said: 'Marry that girl. She is one in a million.' Well I laughed and said to my mum that she was indeed terrific and beautiful but just a girl, so much younger than me. 'Never you mind,' said my mum, but I thought no more of it for some time.

"Then my sister, Olwyn, who is also my literary agent, came to visit from Paris and organized a dinner party. Olwyn was very attractive and a bit of a party girl, very worldly, very outspoken, and she invited a number of her sophisticated friends and included Carol, perhaps wanting to get to know her. Perhaps Mum had said something. It was a warm summer's night and the party got very wound up with wine and storytelling and a lot of verbal toing and froing among the guests. Carol remained stonily silent throughout. Then at one point, Olwyn turned to her, saying something like: 'And what do you have to say for yourself?' And Carol, apparently completely intimidated by the older, much worldlier guests around her, fainted dead away right at the table.

"Of course everyone was shocked, and I gathered her up in my arms and carried her out to give her some air. I set her on the grass in the moonlight and stroked her forehead and, gazing at her, her long black hair, pale skin and lovely features in repose, I fell in love with her."

For a moment the grizzled bush-worn assembly falls silent. We are all deeply touched, and so I propose a toast to Carol. Ted smiles deeply and raises his glass: "My true salvation." A great story, whether true or poetic apocrypha. But does it matter? I wonder.

. . .

MY NEPHEW MARK Dayneka greets us upon our return to Vancouver. Mark's a lovely gentle soul who somehow has survived his mother's being totally paralyzed with Guillain-Barré syndrome during her pregnancy with him, being pushed into a campfire by my boisterous daughter Jennifer when they were infants, a near fatal mauling by the family coon hound, being run over by a car while riding a Ski-Doo and several attacks by marauding grizzly bears in the Canadian Arctic where he worked as a geologist. He is staying with us and attending Simon Fraser University, hoping to become a biologist and spend more time in civilization. It sounds like a prudent plan. He tells us he has spotted some steelhead lying in deep pools in the nearby Seymour though the river is dead low from the late summer drought, just the opposite of the Dean farther north, where the autumn rainstorms have struck with a vengeance.

After a day of recuperation, we decide to hike to see for ourselves. The Seymour, having for more than fifty years been kept in isolation from most intruders—only those with a fisherman's special permit were allowed entry—is truly a journey through the looking glass. The river flows through a fairly tony neighbourhood with giant trees and shaded pools and riffles until, in North Vancouver, it enters an estuary sadly modified by industry that nevertheless still teems with marine life. At the remote, north end is a bower where I have on occasion encountered deer, black bear and, once, even a cougar. It is a lost world of derelict bridges and abandoned farms and logging chutes retaken by the rainforest.

We tramp along in our shorts and wading boots, having forsaken waders to traverse the stream bare-legged during the heat of the autumn afternoon. At the shingle bolt, a huge bathtublike pool at the base of a round bald granite rock, we spot a school of coho swirling in such impeccable unison they appear to be a single entity. But in the glare of the sun, they ignore our flies. Then Ted puts on a tiny Ally's Shrimp, an orange "hot" fly with an impossibly long tail, all the rage in the U.K. Standing well back from the edge he drops the fly with a light cast into the pool, letting it sink deep, then starts to strip in line frantically. Sure enough one fish peels away from the squadron and attacks. For several seconds it flashes about the pool and then suddenly scurries back to its mates. As I have discovered fishing with Ted in many different circumstances, he is one of those true anglers: not the best caster, not a fly tier, not a rod techie, not even an aggressive wader, but someone who will catch fish if anyone can. A fish hawk. Only a few of my friends have the knack. (Unfortunately, I do not.) Ted retrieves the fly to discover the hook has broken and, upon tying on another, makes several casts, but the school of coho, as is often their inclination, has developed lockjaw.

We push on upstream to the first cribbing of logs laid horizontally long ago to stabilize the stream bank. As we watch from the hill above, we spot two steelhead. But our shadows spook them as we descend and they vanish into the depths. At the farm gate, the entrance to an old homestead, I put Mark into "the bucket"—that is, the right position to lay a fly over the hold, the traditional resting place of a summer steelhead, where an icy spring-fed stream pours into the pool over a rock face, cooling the heated summer river water. Ted and I watch in silence. Mark makes one, two casts covering the silky smooth epidermis of the pool with his drifting dry fly. On the third, a mighty bulge swells behind his fly as a steelhead rolls, eyes it, declines. It is all the action we are to have that day but it is enough. Ted is charmed by the place, taken by its magical transformative nature— a wilderness river right next to the city. Perhaps the aquatic version of a poem? I remember his description of the method for hunting down a poem in his wonderful how-to book *Poetry in the Making*. In the book, intended for use in schools, Ted describes how writing a poem is like capturing an animal.

One must know its essence and true nature and be very precise. And then it becomes easy, as you think like the animal and can predict where it will go, how it will behave and how you can catch it. But you must be exacting in your preparation. So too with a poem. It makes no sense to embellish a thought. One must merely capture the essence of it in a few words and the poem will appear. And indeed the Seymour does intensify and focus our experience in stark contrast to the transitory nature of the suburb through which we drove to get here. Not to mention its restorative qualities, allowing us to be yanked out of our everyday lives so quickly and easily. Refreshing our spirits and allowing us, to risk a pun, to see more.

That evening Lee Straight calls to suggest that we spend the next day fishing the Coquihalla, a hallowed summer steelhead stream near the town of Hope that like so many others suffered overkill until anglers and government biologists realized that steelhead numbered only in the hundreds, at best a thousand or so. It was just their willingness to attack a lure or fly that made them seem so numerous in the bad old days of killing as many as possible. Most recently the Coquihalla has suffered the indignities caused by the building of the highway of the same name and then multiple crossings in the laying of a gas pipeline. But the river remains a delicate, crystal clear mountain stream that figures prominently in the legend of B.C. steelheading, for one of the province's most prominent early angling artists, Tommy Brayshaw, made his home on the river at Hope, and Haig-Brown himself used to

visit. To fish it is a pilgrimage. In 1946, a group of prominent Vancouver citizens led by Gardner Frost and Cornelius
Burke hosted a weekend of drinking, eating, playing bridge
and even fishing that came to be known tongue-in-cheek as
La Société des Sieurs Pêcheurs Coquihalliens. The group, now
largely populated by the sons of the originals, still meets, but
on Vancouver Island, fishing mostly the Stamp and Gold
rivers of the West Coast.

On the way to meet Lee we stop in a local fly-fishing
shop to buy some flies, and the local expert, Kelly David-
son, a fine flyfisher and tier, takes Ted aside and hands him a
"secret killer fly." I can't believe my eyes. It is a Greaseliner-
type fly, one intended to be fished in the surface film where it
can bob and weave and create a commotion. But it is gargan-
tuan, humbling in size even my grotesque Thompson River
Rats. And the Thompson is one of the largest rivers in British Columbia, whereas the Coquihalla is a lovely, tumbling
mountain stream.

"That fly will look like a waterlogged chicken in that
rocky little creek!" I protest.

"Just try it," whispers Kelly conspiratorially.

"I will indeed," says Ted, thrilled to be given an edge in
the proceedings.

"I saw what he gave you," says Mark and instantly pur-
chases a couple.

I don't cover myself in glory on the drive up, for as we
approach Chilliwack, my truck dies. I have forgotten to
fill it with gas. So I hitchhike to the station only a couple of

kilometres ahead, rationalizing that it will give Mark, Lee and Ted an opportunity to get to know one another. We are delayed an hour and Lee is muttering about losing the best part of the day. But soon we are at the section known as Othello. The river comes off the steep mountains that separate the Interior from the Pacific and, though the area was logged over a hundred years ago, the trees have returned. A bower of cottonwoods and Douglas firs lines the river, providing something of a canopy and shade for the insects and fish of the tumbling emerald stream that flows to join the Fraser. The river is so transparent, we literally have to creep towards the bank, lest we spook any fish lying in the pools. Our hopes are not high: the midday sun is beating down, so we opt for lunch and a beer at Iago. Ted loves the Shakespearean allusions associated with the Kettle Valley Railway that used to follow the river. I describe how the engineer who named the stations was a great admirer of Shakespeare and even lectured in the evenings to the railroad building crews on the different plays with which each stop is associated. Ted volunteers that Shakespeare is his favourite writer and that no one in any language has equalled his creations. He adds that he is writing a book in which he argues that in most of Shakespeare's tragedies there is one basic story: hostility between father and son, with, sometimes, the complicating factor of the mother figure. He says it has taken him several hundred pages to lay out his analysis of the ancient archetypal acts and symbols of violence, conflict and resolution among humankind and he hopes to be done in another year.

"Poetry sounds much less painful, Ted," I observe.

"God yes," he says. "I don't know why I am driven to write that book. It may kill me."

On a blanket we lay out lunch, a spread of smoked meats, Asiago and Gouda cheeses, garlic pickles, summer-sweetened tomatoes, heavy rye bread, grapes, peaches and apples, while we sip on *hefeweizen*—wheat beer that has been cooling on ice during our two-hour journey. Lee can't stand the indolence of the picnic and after a few bites is gone upstream. Ted takes his cue and, picking up his rod, ambles over to a bend in the river only about a hundred metres away. As with much of fishing, the setting justifies the trip with snow-capped mountains in the background, aspens rattling in the breeze and the summer sun transforming the water into the constantly changing light of a flowing stained-glass window. It is surpassingly beautiful but Mark and I, given the brilliant sunshine, linger over our lunch, thinking all we will get is casting practice. Within twenty minutes Ted lets out a shout as a ten-pound silver steelhead cartwheels down the pool. We are amazed but pleased, and I arrive just as Ted is ready to beach it. He wears the Cheshire grin of a successful mouser when Lee arrives and asks about the commotion. Lee is dubious, but I point out I have taken pictures.

Farther north, at Portia, there is more cover from a grove of cottonwoods and firs, and I challenge Ted to repeat his success in the turbulent riffle before us, explaining that in warm weather steelhead like to lie behind or in front of rocks where there is a surfeit of oxygen.

We are flabbergasted when within a dozen casts Ted is once again fast to a ghostly bright-white doe of eight to ten pounds that makes one long run, taking out all of his flyline and even some backing line. Two porpoising leaps and it is coaxed to the beach.

. . .

RETURNING TO VANCOUVER, some time later the four of us—Vicky, Alexei, Ted and I—decide to head up to the Thompson River to check out the trout fishing. There won't be steelhead until October, but Ted is keen nonetheless, since his previous trip was overshadowed by the bout of appendicitis and surgery. This time we head up to an area just below Black Canyon, a dark forbidding section of whitewater encased in rock that appears to be the charred, excreted bowels of an ancient volcano. It lies just downstream of Ashcroft, a charming cowboy town that was once the gateway for mule trains that supplied the Cariboo gold rush in the early 1860s. Although Ashcroft experienced a devastating fire in 1916, it still retains much of its early frontier architecture, as well as a rich history involving characters of both indigenous and European origin. It is the hometown of several prominent ranches and even has a recently renovated opera house that hosts surprisingly high-quality musical acts, though usually leaning more to the folksy roots genre than the classical.

I am negotiating with a farmer to buy some acreage here and eventually build a cabin. It is an unusual spot for the

Thompson Valley for there are no railway tracks or roads on either bank of the river, just a dense grove of magnificent ponderosa pines, cottonwoods, aspens and the largest junipers I have ever seen. Nests of songbirds, hawks and eagles abound. Crossing through grassland meadows of wild asparagus and desert silver and Russian rye grass, where herds of huge mule deer sequester themselves to birth their babies, one comes to another grove of trees that lines the river for more than a mile.

In June, rare and exquisite pink and yellow sagebrush mariposa lilies bloom. Yellow and orange prickly pear cactus flowers are everywhere among the rabbit brush and sage. The cluck of partridge echoes between the desiccated hills that rise from the broad valley to verdant forest at a couple of thousand feet and eventually to nearly seven thousand. The valley bottom is a microclimate within the arid surroundings and is extraordinarily fertile, thanks to the river's flooding during the spring freshet. Encamped by the river, I often pinch myself that I am not back in the matinee westerns of my childhood. The real world seems very far away.

Desperadoes really did ride these hills. Perhaps most famous among them were Bill Miner, known as The Grey Fox, an American who in the early 1900s pioneered robbing trains after stagecoaches became passé, and the marauding McLean Gang, who killed some local ranchers before being taken in a gun battle near Douglas Lake in the late 1870s. All of the McLean Gang, including a sixteen-year-old, were hanged in New Westminster.

During the railroad building of the 1880s, Americans brought more than twenty thousand cattle into the area, overgrazing the hills and allowing the sagebrush to flourish. Cattle ranches still thrive, for the desert silver grass is nutrient rich.

We camp on an island with the permission of my friend Bob Pasco, chief of the local Oregon Jack Creek Band and an amazing fellow, a chemistry graduate from Eastern Washington University, and with his wife, Sandy, an accomplished rodeo competitor. Their ranch in Ntaquem near Ashcroft is so fastidiously maintained you can practically eat off the ground in their corrals. The band claims the island as part of its reserve lands but Bob allows us to camp there and to serve as stewards, warding off trespassers. It is a sandy atoll that is inundated by flood waters in the spring but in September makes ideal camping, away from the din of the railways with only the whispering sounds of the teal blue Thompson penetrating the silence of the desert. Across the river we watch two ospreys teach their young to fish. I lead Ted over to view a huge eagle's nest in a towering ponderosa. Two eaglets sitting in the nest look over at us. At that moment, a bizarre event occurs. An osprey with a trout in its talons flies over and hovers above the nest, crying plaintively and apparently taunting the eaglets, then takes off when the adults show up. Ted, some of whose poetry has been characterized as anthropomorphic, is astounded by this humanlike display of pride and gratuitous scorn.

Sipping gin and tonics laced with lime and fresh strawberries, we put together our rods. Unlike those for steelheading, these are light, willowy single-handers used mainly for casting dry flies that are tied to resemble adult stone flies creeping onto the rocks, sedges hatching at the river's surface and unfortunate grasshoppers blown into the stream. Unlike steelhead, which feed only sporadically after entering the river (we were constantly told by biologists that steelhead, especially winter steelhead, feed only vestigially; that is, not for sustenance but only occasionally as a conditioned response—a falsehood contradicted by years of observation), the trout eat almost continually in the autumn to grow and store up fat for the meagre winter months. The fishing can be frantic, or frustratingly slow if the barometer drops or the trout key onto something we still haven't identified.

After the sun cools ever so slightly, we head upstream about five hundred metres. There the riffle pours into a deep, long pool with the seam of current moving off towards midstream, leaving a slower, almost slack area through which we wade, casting our flies. It is in this slower water that dozens of mighty chinook salmon—up to thirty and even forty pounds—dig nests called redds and await spawning. Surrounding them, in the fall in odd-numbered years, there are hundreds of pink salmon. The trout move into those prime staging spots to feed on the roe that the fish eventually deposit in their nests, even bumping into them to induce some premature ejaculation if they can get away with it.

Thus a fly with some weight in it, created to look like a fish egg, can be deadly efficient, though once again I prefer to fish the dry fly, so you can actually see the trout rise, and feel it mouth and take your fly. When the trout are on a rampage targeting insects floating downriver to their feeding stations, there is no place on earth I would rather be.

It takes Ted only a couple of casts to hook a fish that becomes airborne immediately. He has caught rainbows before but none as powerful and none in such classic western surroundings. He chuckles as he gazes at the iridescent silver, gold and pink of his prize; it's probably only a pound and a half in weight but everything is to scale when you are using such a little rod. We take several smaller fish over the course of the evening, but no large ones. At dusk we return to camp, where Vicky is playing with Alexei and has a fire going. We split open the few trout we caught that happened to bleed and grill them over the coals along with sweet fresh corn, and sip river-chilled B.C. Pinot Gris.

That night my nephew Mark regales us with stories of his encounters with grizzly bears. Ted and Alexei are all ears, but then as Alexei starts to fade he crawls onto Ted's belly. Ted is lying on his back on a makeshift bench, and they look up at the stars while Ted points out the Great and Little Bears and shooting stars flame across the deep unpolluted sky, and Alexei is soon asleep. We continue chatting in low tones, sipping Scotch and wine, not wanting the evening to end. But all things must cease at some point. Two days later we bid

Ted farewell at the airport, making plans for his return the
next year. It has become a tradition.

.   .   .

THE YEAR 1990 is becoming fateful. In February, I am
elected president of the Steelhead Society of British Columbia. I am hoping to put my grand plan for the society into
action, having got my ducks in a row by recruiting a nation-
ally recognized artist (Ken Kirkby), an unimpeachable B.C.
political and social icon (Budge Bell-Irving) and, of course,
the queen's Poet Laureate.

The goals are to create a war chest of renewable funds, to
hire a paid executive director and establish a permanent office,
and to raise the profile of the society with government and
the corporate world. Then we can apply pressure upon government and its fisheries management agencies, especially the
federal Department of Fisheries and Oceans, which, beyond
wonderful scientists and frontline enforcement people, is
peopled by many opportunistic, apparently cynical career-
ists who seem to serve only as the handmaidens of commercial fishing and polluting industries. I recall Ted's comment:
"Remember, Haig-Brown said: 'Rivers need friends' . . . and,
I would add, great rivers need great friends and a great many
friends." He's right. When it comes to conservation, we have
to look beyond our own narrow self-interests.

One element is still missing, however: I need a bright
young entrepreneur, a go-getter with a commitment to fish

and conservation. In parallel, as a criminologist, I want to bring the plight of wild fish and wild rivers to the attention of government, corporations and the public. Ted thinks it is good to yoke the ideas of fish and rivers to larger society; the plight of the environment—unlike the threat of a gun or having your purse snatched—is less immediately frightening, though in the long run no less grave. Then a splendid opportunity affords itself: Globe 90, the first world conference on the environment and business, is slated for Vancouver in March. Some conservation groups show no interest, derogating it as merely an opportunity for government and business to promote so-called technological panaceas.

Ted and I chat on the phone a couple of times a week about the impending environmental crisis, a subject that has tormented him for many years. Back in 1970 Ted had written in a review published in an environmental magazine that the time for conservation had arrived, and that our revelation that the earth is a single organism was not an original thought. Rather, that it was humankind's first extraordinary idea and is the core of most primitive religions. He predicted that science and the computer would reinstate those primitive ideas as most necessary for the sustenance of life and a blueprint for the universe. His sentiments meld perfectly with mine.

I tell Ted my plans for us to combine our ideas—a renewed respect for the mysteries of nature combined with empirical evidence of how our commercial practices (logging stream banks, indiscriminately gillnetting runs of mixed stocks of fish, relying on the techno fix of hatcheries and, even worse, fish farms rather than restoration of natural spawning beds) are destroying the natural healing qualities of the earth—and I am practically bubbling over in anticipation of his next visit. In the meantime, I prepare a flow chart of the conditions under which pollution is allowed in society, how government deals with it and how the public reacts under different conditions using my analysis of pulp mills, logging, fisheries and so on. My session at Globe 90, packed with serious men, ends with a cautionary statement that those corporations that try to cut special deals with governments in camera to evade environmental standards and regulations will inadvertently become the first targets of eco-terrorists; that the best protection is to be as transparently law-abiding as possible. The government types react negatively. Looking very uncomfortable, they whinge about how special deals have to be cut to promote industry, employment and the creation of wealth. It is a moment of great disillusionment for me, who always believed that good, conscientious government is the only salvation, but a moment of enlightenment as well.

Ted and I are looking forward to preparing a plan of action when he gets to Vancouver, a future campaign that will come to fruition over a year or two. And to work on the book he has proposed, a picaresque mélange from the history of literature of fishing stories both grandiose and modest, with one simple criterion for inclusion: compellingness. My part, to choose from the North American literature, is already done. But then, a major setback—the first of several waiting in the wings. Ted discovers he must cancel his August visit. I find a replacement for the Dean, but we must put our larger plans on hold. Meanwhile, I am dealing with a bit of a crisis at home. Vicky has been swept up in the net of layoffs at the CBC and her Vancouver show, *Pilot 1*, is cancelled. She becomes depressed as she realizes we will have to give up the house if she can't find another job. At the eleventh hour she does find one with a local production company and rockets from black depression to euphoria. I am relieved. I shouldn't be.

Ted's letter, dated August 15, arrives as we are making plans for the Dean. It is clear that he couldn't take time for the trip this year because his brother and sister-in-law had just spent six weeks visiting. He hadn't seen them for fourteen years—a great but melancholy time of catching up. He describes taking Gerald fishing for sea trout and how he fishes only in the sea in Australia, but spends most of his time golfing, largely to please his wife. He waxes—ironically, given what is soon to follow—about how lucky I am that Vicky enjoys fishing. He rambles on about having to provide some lines of verse for the queen mother's ninetieth birthday, eventually producing 430, to amuse her. Although there is no requirement that he produce any poetry as laureate, he clearly feels a responsibility to do so. Then, as if feeling guilty regarding our project, he comments that he has cleared the time to devote a couple of hours each day to its completion, I having done my part over a year ago. Perhaps most interestingly, he lets slip that since he lectured to a local chapter of the Friends of the Earth on my theory of civil disobedience in the face of threats to the environment and lack of action from government, incidents of eco-terrorism have begun to occur. My theory is not a call to action, rather it focuses on the conditions under which members of the community will be activated through the stages of meeting attendance and letter writing to civil disobedience and beyond, based on the paper I presented at Globe 90 in Vancouver.

He goes on to describe his part in an international competition for writers of plays for children based on environmental themes and then laments a strange crisis in the seas around Britain with sand eels. Until recently they were so plentiful that bays were black with their biomass, now, thanks to their being harvested for food for salmon farms, they are in such short supply that sea birds that feed on them are starving. The surplus catch is used for fertilizer on Russian farms. I can sense the great slow burning anger and despair in his words as he juxtaposes those images.

The trip to the Dean is interesting because there are some opportunities for dry-fly fishing, but water conditions are tough overall and we hook only fifty-four, landing thirty-five. Subpar for us; not bad anywhere else in the world. But there is a big hole in the group with Ted's absence, and we refer to him constantly, to his stories, his large warm reassuring bulk and his quiet boyish enthusiasm as we sit around the campfire. The time is strangely melancholy.

Having taught the summer semester and with Vicky in a new job, I spend the fall researching case studies of polluters. I devote my evenings to Alexei, taking him on river walks, and handling the domestic chores.

Just before Christmas, on our anniversary, I am devastated to discover that my marriage is not what I thought it was. Nothing is more devastating than to discover that the person with whom you think you share a vision of the world is living a parallel life. You try to win her back but all to no effect. I feel as if I am about to vanish into thin air and would welcome that outcome. I am saved only by the constant attention of devoted friends that include Ken Kirkby, John Hamill, Barry Stuart and Ted, whom I call for some commiseration, only to discover he is in deep agony from shingles that have rendered him virtually blind. It is the day after he finished his monumental study, *Shakespeare and the Goddess of Complete Being*. I don't have the heart to burden him with anything other than the barest details of my crisis.

Over the next three months, though, we talk regularly. On the last occasion of my ongoing agony, he explains that he can't be totally frank as there are others in the room, but he offers me some metaphorical advice: "When one lives with wolves, one must be a wolf." During a previous conversation he had said: "He who wishes to understand wolves spends a lot of time staring into the darkness of the forest." I take a lot of time thinking about these parables and contemplating how best to act on them. Everywhere I go, the shadow of Winston Churchill's "black dog" of depression darkens my day.

I bury myself in my projects. Sleep comes only in four-hour spurts and then I spring awake. I lose twenty pounds. But my teaching and my advocacy become strangely energized. I find I am too agitated to pursue any in-depth writing projects beyond an article or a chapter. I speak with Ted every few weeks; slowly, he appears to be recovering from the crippling effects of shingles.

In April he writes and, in his typically charitable and empathic way, tries to present Vicky's point of view for, as he relates, his own experience of obsession is from her perspective, which he reminds me he has referred to in the past. He describes how he has been out of control on two occasions though remaining during and forever after in love with—for him—a person infinitely more significant. He reflects how in retrospect those episodes seem not to have had anything to do with his real relationships, that the first one wrenched him from one world (I presume that of Sylvia) and put him in another (that of Assia Wevill? Sylvia invited her to visit and he had an affair and, eventually, a child with her; in an irony of fate, incredibly cruel, she too killed herself, as well as their child). The second relationship apparently lasted eighteen months but he does not elaborate on it. He goes on to relate that he experienced total separation and loss in the first and in the second, he presumes, total forgiveness. He says he can't be sure Carol did forgive him, but she made him feel as if she had so that they could create a new life, universe, together. He says that he can't say how it would be for the male forgiver. Then, as if overwhelmed by the weight of the topic, slides into good news regarding commissions for my writing that he has a line on with *The Field* and *The Telegraph*.

Ted is right. My job is to re-create the life, the structure, that made us fall in love and commit to one another. I try to think what she loves most in the world: Scotland. We shall

go to Scotland and rediscover one another. I pitch a story to the British Tourist Association: Scottish rivers that support runs of salmon and single malt whiskies. They go for it and provide an exciting itinerary. We leave in September, a desperate last attempt. A letter from Ted awaits us at our first destination, urging me to get hold of the editor of *The Field* ("seems an extremely nice chap"); then Ted launches into a promotion of his secret weapon, the Ally's Shrimp, an orange concoction that has proved a miracle, he suspects, because of its extremely long tail and the specific way it is fished: downstream with an additional downstream mend and a fast strip in order to excite the fish into chasing it. He says that when we fish the Tweed the Duke of Roxburgh will take us out and show us "The Flats," an ideal place for the shrimp, requiring a long Dean-like cast. He ends with the observation that the chief advantage of the shrimp is to tell only your dearest friends about it. In his sweet kind way he is signalling to me his efforts not only to buck up my spirits but to focus on issues of mutual pleasure. And they are having a salutary effect on me.

I am touched by Ted's efforts to cheer me and flattered by his efforts to turn me into a full-time writer. He thinks

I should stop teaching and plunge completely into writing during this time of crisis, a time that can create opportunity by shattering the glass ceiling of complacency.

The British Tourist Authority–hosted trip is rich in experience with visits to the Tweed, Spey and, my favourite, the Tay, and in wonderful single malt Scotch, but not in fish. Not until the last day, when on our own we book a beat on the Borgie. Alexei, Vicky and I all fish the beat—a specific length of river reserved for the day for a specific number of rods—and in the last hour Vicky hooks and lands an eight-to ten-pound salmon that is quite gravid, ready to spawn, and so she releases it. I phone Ted to announce the eleventh-hour triumph. He says we have done better than most anglers fishing rivers in the worst year in memory. I agree. I hope Vicky's landing of that salmon is a sign that the darkest days of our marriage have passed and that, even given the bleak-est prospects, when nothing seems to work, there is hope for resurrection and renewal just as that salmon doomed to die was released and sent on to spawn and renew its line.

6 / RE-CREATION IN
ANCIENT CELTIC LANDS

Our plane is filled with a gaggle of laughing and squealing rosy-cheeked young Londoners. Giddy with each other's company, the gang sip champagne they produced from a handbag and crowd the portholes to eye the desolate Hebridean Isles of the North Atlantic off the west coast of Scotland far below. Their enthusiasm is infectious. Then a gale strikes. The aircraft rattles and rolls, glasses fly amid titters turned to cries of dismay and champagne pours over laps. Finally, the aircraft descends, protesting crankily—as if reeled in on a kite cord—and, none too soon, we are bumping along the tarmac. Spontaneous applause.

Welcome to Stornoway, unofficial capital of the Outer Hebrides and namesake for the official Opposition's residence

in my own capital, Ottawa. It is 1992 and I am on Lewis, the
northern two-thirds of the island of Lewis and Harris. (In
1923 the industrialist Lord Leverhulme granted Lewis to
its inhabitants after they spurned his attempts to redevelop
the island and revolutionize their lives.) The collegiate flock
moves as one through the storm and disappears into the ter-
minal building past a lissome figure in an anorak, blonde hair
pasted to her forehead. She is Debbie Millar, housekeeping
head of Grimersta Lodge. An angel. I am soaked to the skin
in clothes better suited for Italy and very happy to see her.

Just the week before, I had been at a conference in amber-
lit Siena when Ted called. My visit to Devon to fish the Exe
with him was still some days off.

"Ehor, listen carefully. We can stay with the original plan
or tag it on to a rare opportunity. Four extra days have come
up on the Grimersta; would you like to join me and my fishing partner, Bill Tucker?"

"That would be nice," I responded languidly, tracking
my pulse as the salmon-mad homunculus within me did
backflips. Ted had told me about the Grimersta and I knew
how difficult it was to secure fishing on its lochs and streams.
Now here I am in that very place. The fishermen's co-op is
unexpectedly closed so I settle for a waterproof slouch cap
and toque acquired at a local tourist shop. Debbie thinks she
can borrow the rest at the lodge, though she eyes my size
13s dubiously. "I'll even wear sandals so long as I can fish,"
I offer.

On the road to the lodge Debbie tells me the students in Stornoway score among the highest grades in their leaving exams; her own son Campbell, who is a gillie, is attending medical school. "Must be natural selection," I observe, noting in the near impenetrable mist a terrain of rock outcroppings among peat bogs and luminescent green pasture, the rain-lashed lochs the colour and seemingly the texture of quicksilver. Not an easy place to kick back in a loincloth and survive plucking fruit from the vine.

"The weather is so harsh that, until quite well into the twentieth century, some locals still inhabited black houses, stone dwellings with no windows at all," continues Debbie. I guess all of that reading by candlelight undistracted by the bright lights produces those scholars. Monks would love it here.

The lodge is a charming, no-nonsense Scottish country house, built in the mid-nineteenth century, not overly large, situated right on the shores of Loch Roag, a sea loch where, if lucky, you can spot shoals of salmon staging for their ascent to the spawning grounds. The fishery is a series of lochs connected by short rivers over many kilometres. In my estimation, it is a perfect combination of spawning and rearing habitat, recognized nearly a century ago by the syndicate of anglers who purchased it from Leverhulme to operate as a private club. One with a very long waiting list.

As an add-on guest, one with the prudence of a long-time denizen of lodges, I first duck into the kitchen to say

hello to the young ladies chatting animatedly as they prepare
the evening meal. Upstairs I park my gear in a comfortable
room overlooking the loch. I grab my camera and, rummag-
ing through the wet room downstairs, upon Debbie's urging
abscond with a pair of size 12 wellies that fit perfectly. I slog
upriver to the Old Bridge Pool, buffeted by wind and rain;
on closer inspection in the low light I marvel at how the river
keeps its clarity as it hurtles serpentine through the peat
meadows. There John Gordon has been "flogging the water"
to no avail, and I move on to where Christopher Butterworth,
a rather stolid but kind fellow, architect and president of the
Flyfishers of London, is experiencing better luck, having
raised several fish and landed two grilse (salmon yearlings)
of four and six pounds.

I wander back down to the lodge just as the rods arrive
from their beats. The first is Ted, looking even more like a
piece of landscape on the loose than I remember—large,
boisterous and welcoming, not the shy, gently quiet fellow
who usually visits me in Canada. Is this what he is like on
his own turf, or is this what he is like when the salmon fishing is good? I don't have time to ponder as he grabs me in an
embrace, practically lifting me off the ground.

"You made it! So good to see you. Your timing couldn't be
better, the fishing has really come on!" Ted rattles on about
how this fishery, traditionally the greatest in Scotland, had
come up against hard times but this year is producing phe-
nomenally, not only in number but in size as well. "Have you

heard of Orri Vigfússon, the Icelander who made a fortune marketing vodka?" He pauses to chuckle. "He has mounted a one-man campaign to save wild Atlantic salmon, taking on most of the blackguards doing their best to destroy our fish: the commercial fishers, the salmon farmers, the drift netters. He is buying out the Faroe Islanders, the worst of the lot. Though I don't trust them. They may take the money and the fish. But he is astounding and I am doing everything I can to help him; one man in the face of governments unwilling to do anything with all their billions." Ted's animated performance startles me: his voice swings seamlessly between a booming bass on the high notes and hissing vitriol when discussing the villains. I look forward to getting to know this Ted Hughes.

With that, John Gordon and Ted's friend Bill Tucker, a very jolly, handsome fellow in his fifties, arrive carrying salmon of twenty-one and nineteen pounds to choruses of oohs and aahs. Very few fish of that size show up in this fishery and to have two of them caught on the same day is extraordinary. Ted declares me a good omen.

"Jury's still out on that," says Peter Squire, a stocky, strong-looking surveyor from Yorkshire whose business is to call everyone on everything, I discover, but who always has a twinkle in his eye. John, being top rod, has to provide champagne for everyone at tea. It is a sweet chore for him: "I needed a victory right about now." Ah, yes, salmon as salve for the souls and egos of men. I understand perfectly.

Writing

TOP: Preparing the laureate spaghetti sauce

BOTTOM: Serving it up

TOP: Choosing the right fly, Ted and Jay on the Dean
BOTTOM: Ted with steelhead

TOP LEFT: Tiny Black Squire—deadly salmon fly on the Grimersta River
TOP RIGHT: Joe Saysell and Ted playing coho off Nitinat on the Pacific
BELOW: A great day's fishing on the Grimersta River

TOP: Ted with steelhead

BOTTOM: Ted with Ehor returning to civilization, 1995

TOP: Georgia's 1st birthday: Alexei, Christian Baker, Jennifer Calvert (née Boyanowsky), Georgia Rose, Ted BOTTOM: Erik Rutherford and Leilah Nadir read the poem "Bride and Groom Lie Hidden for Three Days" at Thea and Sam's wedding. Leilah, Erik, Nethan Hendrie, Sam Anson, Thea Boyanowsky, Shanon Densmore and G. G. Anson

Alas, my aching desire to wet a line is not soon to be assuaged, for the dictates of a strict Free Church disallow fishing on Sundays; there will be none the next day. Ironically, the skies are sunny and still, perfect for casting a line, but we settle for a drive in Bill's Land Rover to Amhuinnsuidhe Castle, which is south on Harris. We pass through terrain so Bergmanesquely bleak it breaks your heart. The castle is a marvellous turreted edifice built in 1867 and added onto by Charles, the seventh Earl of Dunmore, eventually bankrupting him. According to Ted the lower two lochs have recently been polluted by salmon farms but the rest still produce many wild salmon. Ted strikes up a conversation with a passerby, an ancient gillie who says the fishing is good but no one expected it, so no anglers are about. His claim that two rods took ninety salmon a couple of weeks ago raises my eyebrows to new heights. Back home at the lodge, we discuss the next three days' fishing over a lunch of roast beef and Yorkshire pudding, go for a walk to the bridge, snooze in front of the fire, prepare equipment and enjoy an evening meal of lobster amid much revelry and storytelling.

Dawn cracks across the low hills, bathing them in yellow light. The silky surface of the loch looks much more inviting this morning. After a hearty breakfast of porridge and toast, Ted and I head out, I in a Barbour borrowed from Peter that I may not need today. We have both Campbell Millar and Jason Laing for gillies, the latter sporting a black eye, apparently a souvenir from an altercation in the pub the night before. The boys know their history, telling us how the island was originally Norwegian but was given to James I as a wedding present for his marriage to Anne of Denmark, second daughter of Frederick II, king of Denmark and Norway. Alexander McLeod became the local laird sometime later but, like the Earl of Dunmore, went bankrupt and sold it to James Matheson, who in turn sold it to Lord Leverhulme. I had no idea bankruptcy was such an occupational hazard among the local aristocracy.

"No one is immune around here," declares Ted. "It isn't easy to eke out a living on these isles, though many have tried to make their fortunes here."

"How about writing? Not many distractions."

"Too much time spent merely surviving. Everything becomes more important than the scribbling one is supposed to get around to. But the fishing is good."

"The main export is brains," says Jason.

We ride in the runabout with several others who are dropped off at various beats until we get to the head, where the outlet stream pours into the lake. We fish fourteen-foot double-handed rods with floating lines and a bright-blue grey-and-white-winged fly, the Elver, as a dropper or attractor. On the business end our gillies recommend very small midge-type flies, which to a North American salmon angler appear microscopic, or hairy streamer light tubes. I put on a MacCleay Bucktail Streamer. At MacCleay's Pool, we stand on the shore of the loch at the outlet of a stream and cast into it: nothing. I leave Ted and wander down to Bill, who is fishing a spot called Sanderson's. He is elated, having had four fish on and just as I arrive Campbell is netting his second landed, of ten pounds. I walk back to Ted in time to see him pulling himself out of the stream drenched but still fast to a feisty salmon that leaps about while he rights himself, chuckling thankfully, and lands it, nine-and-a-half pounds. I am feeling decidedly goatlike.

Then Jason suggests a very curious thing: that Ted and I get into a rowboat on the loch and sit at the stern while he rows into the wind.

"What is this, Ted?" I inquire, slightly embarrassed. "A last-ditch effort to help the hapless colonial?"

"No, no," Ted protests, "standard procedure worked out over a hundred years. Just take this single-handed rod. I am putting on a muddler minnow as a dropper—

"Invented in Canada," I interject, trying to salvage some national pride.

"—and attach this tiny fly that Peter claims is his secret weapon: the Black Squire."

"You must be joking. It's one-quarter the size of my thumbnail," I comment, bemused.

"It's what works here. Just go ahead," Ted counsels.

"I'm in your hands," I sigh. I cast out about fifty or sixty feet, and Jason pulls on the oars. I see the fly lift and, amazingly, within a few strokes a salmon follows, showing its full length.

"There she is." My rod dips ever so slightly.

"Strike," shouts Jason, and I am fast to a good-sized silver hen fish that cartwheels above the lake. Ted is elated: "Well done! Keep a tight line but take your time."

I have taken more than a few salmon but never quite in this manner. Jason is heaving mightily, trying to keep the fish from running through the outlet and into the stream, which apparently can portend disaster. Fortunately the fish is soon content to come to the net and I have my first Grimersta salmon, an especially fine specimen at thirteen-and-a-half pounds.

Ted takes up the rod and fishes for some time and then graciously insists I take another turn, though I protest it is his until he hooks another. He won't hear of it, so I take the rod, reel in about ten feet and astoundedly am soon into another.

"Now you've got the magic," he chuckles. His magnanimity is rewarded after lunch in the fishing hut, when he wanders over to an area that the seasoned anglers deride as unproductive and immediately nails a small fish. Within minutes he has two more takes. It is becoming clear that we are witnessing the characteristic arrival of Grimersta fish in large shoals. I wander up to the loch shore and cast towards the outlet. A fish comes to the fly, head and tail, but misses. Two more times. But on the fourth, I have him, a leaper of six pounds.

As we ride down the loch, basking in glory, I comment to Ted that this has matched my best first day ever on a salmon fishery. "I imagine the waiting list for the club is long. Do most people get in after a few years as guests?"

"Not everyone. One mercurial guest hooked a very large fish at the outlet with Jason here on the oars and started screaming apoplectically at him to pull away, pull harder . . . rather unpleasant. Caused a bit of a commotion that several members witnessed. When he landed the fish and calmed down, he realized he'd been out of line and so asked Jason, clearly trying to patch things up, what he would like to do in his career. Jason's reply was 'Go away, make a lot of money and join the club, so I can come back and shout at the gillies!' The fellow was struck from the list." We all laugh, none more than Jason himself.

It looks like champagne will be our treat, but we are greeted by a very upbeat Peter Squire. "How many?"

"Eight landed, many more hooked among the three of us. And you?"

"Eight landed, and Francis here took five more. Maybe you aren't all bad luck, Ehor. Champagne all around's on me."

The next day we are out before breakfast in a howling gale. I am standing on the rocky shore in the lower pools making long casts with the big rod, when once again the Black Squire connects and I land a ten-pounder. Ted has none, but Bill has already landed a similar-sized fish so, cold and hungry, we head back to the lodge. After a hearty repast, Ted is out again like a flash and is rewarded with two fresh salmon, and Bill takes two others on the river. At day's end I tag into a manky cock fish that everyone tells me must have been feeling sorry for me.

On the last day we are greeted by a surpassingly beautiful dawn sky streaked with copper and violet and we fish the lower river bathed in sunlight. Ted hits three fish in the Major's Pool, landing none. After breakfast I venture to the outlet of the first loch and, standing among shoulder-high bushes, make a long cast to the lip. A fish immediately rises, head and tailing on my fly but eventually rejecting it. A second cast and as the fly passes the spot there is a slight pluck, but fortunately I don't strike so she is not pricked. On the third cast she takes and, even though she proves to be only four pounds, I am delighted as we are able to witness the whole process. That last evening a strange awkwardness arises between our group—now relegated to a small side table—and the new group who preside at the main. But it is Peter who has the last word when a "new boy" asks about the fishing.

"Sixty-three salmon to twenty-one pounds landed; many more lost. Not bad."

"Not bad, indeed!" the main table crowd is suddenly silent—in respect, we choose to believe. Our group resumes its merrymaking with renewed vigour, the pecking order properly restored.

· · ·

THE FOLLOWING DAY we arrive at Mellands, Bill Tucker's home in Devon. It's a large pink Georgian house nestled on three acres among trees and flowers in an extremely serene setting of great oak trees. Sue, Bill's wife, also serene and very welcoming, is the perfect doyenne in the environs. There to greet us as well is Ted's wife, Carol, whom I've been looking forward to meeting but not without a little trepidation. She is tall, raven-haired and fair-skinned, very attractive. The quintessential strikingly handsome British countrywoman with a commanding presence and manner. I can understand how Ted fell in love with her on that fateful evening when she was barely more than a girl. I feel like a schoolboy as she skewers me with her gaze and, upon spotting the cameras slung on my shoulder, announces they are not to be used at Court Green. "Your wish is my command," I sputter.

After drinks and snacks we head for North Tawton, a traditional West Country village of narrow streets and row houses. The countryside comprises many rolling fields and some low hills with scattered copses of trees. The streets and roads are largely deserted and, as Ted points out various landmarks, Roman and mediaeval, I can visualize the Roman legion that haunts the area, marching over the hills in the moonlight. In fact the air is thick with ghosts, history.

Ted opens the gate in the venerable taupe-toned stonewall to Court Green and we drive in. We enter through an ancient structure, perhaps once a portcullis, into a large courtyard of stones laid on edge by prisoners of the Napoleonic wars. It is not what I expected—too tidy and stylish to be Ted's. The house to the right, huge and immaculately coiffed with magnificent grey thatching, glows in brand spanking new white paint. To the near left are former stables and Nicholas's printing facilities forming the proximal arm of a *U*. Across the courtyard what turns out to be Ted's lair or "junk" room forms the other arm, with a field at the open end facing the doorway to the house. The entrance is positively intimidating, with a great door that appears old enough to be original equipment (twelfth century). Even with its metre-thick walls, the interior is surprisingly bright and warm. Tile, old wood and carpeting are combined on the floor for an extremely stylish though casual aspect. A shiny Aga stove presides over the kitchen. Towards the back there is a great room, post and beam in construction and washed in light from high, well-placed windows, that serves as the main room for entertainment. It is clearly Carol's house.

My room is cosy with a great duvet on the bed and a small tattered copy of lectures by Federico García Lorca obviously intended for me to discover. Back downstairs Carol hands me a glass of fine claret and I wander across the stones, revelling in the antiquity of the place. Through an open door I hear Ted beckoning me: "Ehor, come into the den of the beast if you dare." The long dark building is replete with papers, fishing gear and more papers and books stacked and strewn as far as the eye can see. Ted's world: I have never seen chaos on such an epic scale. Standing behind a huge stack of books and Xeroxed papers, Ted continues: "I wanted to show you that I was indeed working on our book project. I have felt like a truant schoolboy since you finished your part so quickly."

"Do you really write here?" I ask. This is the house of Ted I somehow expected, rather than the elegant abode I have just come out of.

"Of course not, there is too much chaos. This is my repository and research archives and Brobdingnagian gear stash. Come with me."

I follow him into the garden towards the back, facing the church for which his house had served as manse. There, on stilts, is what looks for all the world like a treehouse or playhouse. A single room with only a lamp.

"This is where I work, and you must find a similar place away from the phone and family and friends if you want to finish the big projects. Otherwise, the tendrils reach out and surround you and drag you away, every day, as certain as the seasons come and go. And suddenly you are old and no project is so important anymore."

That evening, Carol and Ted take me to the George Hotel in Hatherleigh, a charming pub and restaurant similar in design to their own home though not quite as stylish. More very good claret, a fine sirloin steak and linguine pesto. The conversation revolves around children. Carol comments that they need unlimited amounts of affection and devotion and that understanding their contradictions is vital. "For example," she says, referring to Frieda and Nicholas, "they may claim they don't care whether you can make it to an important school function or may even say they don't want you to come. But deep down they are relieved if you do."

I agree, thinking of Thea, whom I raised as a single dad for a couple of years before Vicky came on the scene, and how I might have blown it a few times when appointments conflicted but I usually tried to be at the sporting events, grads, and so on. And in fact enjoyed them. It is clear from the survival stories of youthful rebellion that Ted and Carol's children were the centre of their lives.

Back at Court Green, Ted and I sip Scotch and discuss writing. "It is like training for the Olympics," he says. "If I get sidetracked or take a break or go on a trip, it takes me two weeks to get back in the rhythm. I have to go to my hut and my desk and sit there until the juices start to flow. I don't know how you can teach and do your academic politicking for universities and advocacy for the environment and conservation for rivers and still get writing done. I think you have been spinning your wheels. Just give up the university, disappear and only surface when you have a manuscript. I believe you have something to say and that you can do it. You're not indispensable. Others will pick up the slack.

"By the way, I left a book of essays by Lorca on your bed. Look at the one on *duende*. Let's discuss it tomorrow."

Sipping my dram of single malt, I start to read Lorca's essays. I have always been interested in the tragic figure of

the star-crossed poet executed by the Fascists in Franco's
Spain but had never read his essays. He doesn't disappoint.
In his *La teoría y juego del duende*, he writes:

> Manuel Torres... made his splendid pronounce-
> ment: 'All that has dark sounds has *duende*.' And there
> is no greater truth. These dark sounds are the mystery,
> the roots thrusting into the fertile loam known to all of
> us, ignored by all of us, but from which we get what is
> real in art.

To me it sounds like the creative energy that Ted told
me about when describing his dream at university and that
he wrote about in his poem "The Thought-Fox," an energy
that was in danger of being snuffed out by writing endless
essays of literary criticism and that spurred him on to change
his concentration to anthropology.

I rise after a night of my own wild dreams—strange
goblinlike creatures, nuclear holocausts, eerie houses—to a
wonderful, hearty English breakfast of free-range eggs and
fat, sinfully juicy sausages and bacon. While we sip thick
creamy mugs of delicious coffee, Ted returns to the subject
of *duende*. And to my inquiry regarding "The Thought-Fox"
he responds enthusiastically: "Yes, exactly. And I believe
that like a pit viper's venom, it is a finite reservoir in each
person, though perhaps not of equal size, and must not be
wasted or transformed into effluent by useless, bloodless

tasks. It is why, Ehor, you must give up the endless, soul-destroying busy work and get down to what you really want to do. Must do."

"What about you, Ted?" I inquire, attempting to deflect the onslaught.

"It has been the unending struggle of my life: to capture the essence of an experience in a poem and to do so one must extricate oneself from everyday life. You know, Ehor, when you are twenty, life seems infinite. You have nothing but time. By the time you are thirty, you feel you must get on with it and accomplish something. By forty, you wonder whether you will ever be able to get done the things you so desperately wish to do. In your fifties, you are in a panic to get as much done as possible. In your sixties, it seems like borrowed time. You wish to squeeze every bit of juice from every second as it could be all you ever get.

"But now, let's go fishing."

We drive to the River Dart, a diminutive stone-strewn mountain stream spilling off the moor in a series of chutes, runs and pocket water much like the Seymour back home. We are greeted at the reservoir by Simon Day, the laird of the river, a pleasant, intense man in his fifties splendidly turned out in his country tweeds. His family owns a square in London. A friend of Conservative notable Michael Heseltine, he is politically very active and a member of both the South West Water Co. Ltd. and the National Rivers Authority. He chats passionately about the plight of rivers as we ascend the stream among huge oak and chestnut trees, greeting the occasional hiker.

Ted and I scan every bit of water for signs of salmon. Behind a Volkswagen-sized boulder, I spot a fin moving in the current. Ted concurs, though Simon is more skeptical. I lay out the fly, a Jock Scott, with the eleven-foot double-hander and a dusky grey head envelops it. Simon is beside himself with excitement and I offer him the rod—after all, it is his fish. Graciously, he won't hear of it, so I scurry after the eight- to ten-pounder as it struggles to make good its escape. Finally it is ready to come in and Simon goes to tail it. Alas, it spots him, slaps its tail on a rock and is gone. Simon is devastated but we assure him we are thrilled to encounter a salmon on his pretty burn. We hike and chat and examine flowers and mushrooms, including one mammoth orange specimen, for more than an hour and, on the way back, Ted spots another fish. Simon can't see it and insists Ted fish for it. A few casts with a red and yellow tube fly, literally feathers and deer hair lashed around a plastic tube, and Ted is fast to it. This time Simon makes good the apprehension and brings to shore a six-pounder, slightly coloured but in fine shape. Simon shakes his head, saying no one has had such a good day for several years. The salmon gods are still smiling.

We return to Court Green, our cheeks ruddy from the brisk breezy afternoon, to be greeted by a house redolent with the rich aromas of red cabbage cooking in wine, cloves, oranges and other fruits, along with venison and poached salmon. Carol has outdone herself with a culinary master-piece for twelve. The talk around the table is largely of our recent trip to Lewis but it is our exploits on the Dart that elicit the most enthusiasm. As with anglers everywhere, nothing is greeted with as much delight as a visitor's success on a local river, especially one where fishing has been difficult lately. The talk, as always, eventually turns to B.C. bear stories, as Ted recounts to the gasps of the assembled our dealings with grizzlies on the Dean.

We rise to a leisurely breakfast, reflect on the assem-bled company of the night before and then head out in Ted's Volvo. As we approach Tiverton to fish the water of Michael Heathcoat Amory, Ted returns to *duende* and how impor-tant it has been to him. "First as a kind of muse, which if I feel is not kindled within me when working on a poem, I dis-card it and begin again. But once I feel it, I struggle until the work is done regardless of how difficult and exhausting it is. Second, as an effect, once the poem is finished and read aloud. But music—not literature—has the most direct con-nection. Think of the power of *Der Ring des Nibelungen* that brings the audience back night after night. The power to move many people regardless of their education or culture—that is the mark of true art. Art with and of *duende*."

We are winding up a long driveway to a great house perched on a sweeping lawn, its aspect reminiscent of a castle keep. We knock on the door and a beautiful, compact, auburn-haired young woman greets us. She is Arabella Heathcoat Amory and she is utterly charming. So too is the morass of boots, shoes and sporting equipment littering the entranceway. Not what you expect to encounter as you enter a stately home. Michael Heathcoat Amory, a tall rangy man of 1950s matinee idol good looks, welcomes us in. His is a family with a long tradition in the area—owners of textile mills in Tiverton—and in Conservative politics. Michael rummages around and finds me a pair of the ubiquitous British boot waders that fits, sort of, and we head for the River Exe. As part of a small syndicate, Michael owns three miles of fishing on it. It is a charming, pastoral meadowland stream of darkish clear water.

We are met by the river keeper, Barry Yeudall, a Devonian in his forties who is quite bravely cheerful despite his constant back pain from an industrial accident. Michael and Ted go off and leave me with Barry to fish a very likely looking, oak shaded, riffly corner pool but to no avail, so we move on to one called Hudson's: a bucolic, southern English country setting complete with giant oaks, gurgling river and its keeper leaning on a tree watching my every move. It feels like little has changed here for centuries. I am abruptly returned to reality by a heavy take on the Ally's Shrimp wet fly I have been swinging through the riffle. My second encounter in England—rather than Scotland—with a salmon. For me a terribly reassuring experience that just about makes my day, despite the disappointment of losing it. Finally we move into the Meadowland Pool where, to my delight, a fish rolls at my fly midway through its swing.

"Try retrieving a bit," suggests Barry, and instantly the fish rushes the fly—and misses. Now I am getting a little shaky as that was a big, bright salmon. Next cast, I switch to a No. 8 Stoat's Tail with a silver body and a blue beard and I retrieve much longer, and this time the fish takes firmly and cartwheels into the sky, a very fine twelve-pound-plus specimen, but comes unhooked. Obviously, as too often happens on the retrieve, it was hooked in the lip rather than in the hinge of the jaw. Only a few minutes later, I hook another that unfortunately—or perhaps, given my lack of success landing them, fortunately—comes to the net rather docilely. I regain a vestige of respectability as a fish catcher, and so Barry now wants me to hook a big, brawling fighter worthy of the strain in this river, but nothing else shows up.

Michael and Ted appear. Ted has landed a silver hen, twin to mine, while Michael raised another. Excellent salmon fishing anywhere but totally unexpected in this context. I comment that life in England, in the right circumstances, could be very agreeable. "But very ordered and predictable," Ted says. "Not like confronting the unknown, the way you do in British Columbia."

"Or Russia," Michael adds, having just come back from the Kola Peninsula where a group of six landed 190 salmon in a week. "Very primitive, almost primeval place, and we roared around in ancient Mikoyan 8 helicopters that are nothing to look at but quite amazing machines."

"Let's go have some lunch," offers Michael. I waddle out of the river not the picture of elegance, rather more reminiscent of the Michelin Man, spewing water like a fire boat, the waders having provided all the waterproofing of a mosquito net. "At least it's not glacial Squamish River water," chuckles Ted.

"Thank God! But those parr swimming around in my trousers were making me uneasy."

Lunch is in the dining room, an elegantly shaded room with high windows through which the filtered autumn light plays over the candlesticks and silver laid out among salmon with mayonnaise served with new carrots, asparagus and turnips. The food is very fresh and good; the Chardonnay, a perfect accompaniment. We finish with coulis with cream and fresh fruit for dessert while Ted and I regale them with the grizzly bear stories of which the British appear not to be able to hear enough. The atmosphere is relaxed, almost languid in the afternoon sunshine now pouring into the room.

After lunch I slide into the first pool of this utterly charming river and am thrilled not to feel cool river water seeping into the legs and crotch of my second set of borrowed waders. But the fish have stopped taking. Ted and Michael have gone to the big, slow pool at the corner. I wander down to the Railway Pool, where only one pluck breaks my afternoon reverie of cast and step. I put on the Ally's Shrimp with its tantalizingly long tail and begin again, higher in the current. Yes! A bright fish picks up the fly and rapidly motors upstream. Again and again, each time I recapture line it hurtles away.

This is a strong fish but it finally comes to hand and, when I beach it on a sandy bar, I am surprised it is only seven or eight pounds. Given its courageous struggle and despite uncertainty regarding the protocol—it is often deemed unseemly in Britain to release a fish, especially a salmon— I take a chance and return it unharmed to the river just as Ted and Michael show up. If he's distressed, Michael betrays no objection. They got nothing. Ted is now convinced that I have some special magic that works in England, for we are catching fish everywhere he takes me, and he says the legend will spread.

Back at Court Green we dine on delicious leftovers of venison and salmon with a dessert of clotted cream and marinated pears. Carol goes to bed early. Ted and I talk far into the night of salmon and steelhead as the apotheosis of anadromous life and of their sad plight and what we can do about it; of the Dean; of the relative appeal of living again in England versus British Columbia; of the struggles in my life and marriage; and, briefly, for Ted appears determined to mention it daily, of the need to write while the fire burns within. I ask Ted whether he is tempted like Michael Heathcoat Amory to go to Russia, where friends of mine have assisted in setting up salmon fishing camps on allegedly fabulous salmon rivers, but he is strangely hesitant. His rugged, powerful physical presence masks an artist's sensitivity. "I fear there may be too many ghosts, wretched souls lingering there, for me to enjoy the experience," he says wistfully.

Even the appeal of the Kola, an area of untouched wilderness rivers until recently entirely off-limits to foreigners as the site of missile silos and nuclear submarine bases, is tainted for him by the slaughter of so many writers, artists, people in general by the Communist regime.

We rise late to the discreet clatter of dishes and the allur- ing aroma of brewing coffee. Coming downstairs, I bid Carol—the vision of freshness and energy—good morning and tell her of Ted's cooking efforts in preparation for the Dean trip years ago. I am rewarded with a hearty laugh as Ted rushes to his own sheepish defence.

After breakfast we head for Exeter in the Volvo, my blood pressure rising each time we sweep around a blind curve at breakneck speed on the single-track, densely hedged back roads. The British are amazing drivers. If such roads existed in Canada there would be carnage for a period and then a huge public outcry to eliminate them, despite their charm.

We arrive at an appealing, slightly timeworn house of lovely simple lines, overlooking a beautifully treed garden and meadow through which the River Exe meanders. In the distance the towers of the University of Exeter line the horizon. A more bucolic setting I have never witnessed. In fact it is what I have dreamed of as the ideal and idyllic situation: a country house with viewpoints through which I can spot fish rising and wander down to cast a fly at leisure.

Ted introduces me to Ian Cook—an art dealer and conservator—who has made a fortune buying and selling obscure paintings by old masters. The owner of fishing in this section of the Exe, he is a soft-spoken, handsome, curly-haired fellow married to Liz, a striking woman in her forties. They have a daughter who is downright beautiful. All things to aspire to and, once achieved, worth fighting for.

As the tale unfolds, I learn Ian has become something of a national hero, having discovered upon buying this extraordinary property of fourteen acres that the river was badly polluted. Dismayed, Ian approached various regulatory agencies only to be turned away by bureaucrats unwilling or unable to do anything about the commercial laundry, textile mill and municipal sewage system that dumped waste directly into the river. Ian decided to look into the law himself and, possibly with the help of legal scholars and certainly the encouragement of Ted, discovered ancient British common law that declared a man has a right to demand that the water flowing past his property be unpolluted. Against the advice of several lawyers Ian undertook a series of wildly risky but ultimately successful court cases, forcing the polluters to clean up their discharge.

Attesting once again to an infinitely forgiving and resilient Mother Nature, the salmon and trout have returned to his section of river. Thank God for British common law. And so we go down into the meadow, where we see some large fish rising and I watch Ian on one knee stalk the holding fish and cast elegantly. Then I try my hand as well but with no success, so we repair to the deck for tea.

As has become our custom, we talk late into the night after returning to Court Green. Ted is fascinated by the duality of the human psyche: the rational that aspires to achieve success in business, academia and government, and to get married and protect the nest; and the bestial or animal part that is irrational and, when totally activated, becomes obsessed. Ted is especially interested when I recount the recent findings of neuropsychology, and he relates them to the strange experiences he has in great supply. 155

"Tell me what you think of this," he begins. A very beautiful woman, educated and with all the opportunities of the world, became enslaved to a cultish black figure. She followed him around, avoided contact with her family, became little more than a pet animal serving and servicing him, apparently in contentment. Her desperate parents tried the authorities and psychiatrists, everyone. "Finally they brought in a white witch who literally ripped open her soul with her bare hands and she escaped, awakened, came to her senses and felt she had just vacated a nightmare."

"How did you know her?"

"Through friends. And she took a liking to me but then a strange thing happened. One night I recounted how, while serving in the R A F at a remote radar base, several of us young recruits came to observe spiders fighting and, to amuse ourselves, we would pit them against each other. It became our main preoccupation. We grew fascinated by them and their combats were so intricate and vicious that we even became strangely sexually aroused as we watched them in their struggles. When she heard that story she became obsessed with me. What do you make of that?"

"Well, I hate to de-romanticize the story, but psychologists would probably identify her as a borderline personality. Someone who does not have a well-developed sense of self and self-worth so gloms on to the most powerful stimulus in the environment whether an idea, a religion or a person, especially a man. Her relationships with women would swing from someone being her very best friend to then being totally devalued, hardly existing or even becoming disparaged, an enemy. She would have a history of short-term friendships.

"But the human mind itself is so fascinating and complex, it isn't as if there is no mystery left. I think the mind will be the last frontier we really get to know, even after outer space."

Ted is a little contemplative the next morning. He tells the story of Stephen Spender, a left-wing poet whose biography by an allegedly friendly writer became a disastrous revelation of his private sex life and homosexual affairs even though he also had a wife and children. I wonder if it is not intended as a cautionary tale akin to the ban on photography imposed by Carol. He does know I keep a journal and so, I presume, it is a plea to be prudent.

We head to Popham's Deli, apparently the best inexpensive small restaurant in England. The food is simple and excellent, with great local cheeses, meats and very fresh vegetables, my favourite ploughman's-type lunch to eat streamside. Then to their farm, where Ted worked with Carol's father and where their experiences became the grist for *Moortown*.

Ted drives me to the train in Exeter. It has been just what I needed in a trip: renewal and re-creation. Re-creation as a father and, now, grandfather to my daughter's newborn in London; as an academic in Siena; as an adventurer in Scotland experiencing the most exotic fishing. And in close friendship in Devon with my dear and great friend Ted. We exchange our sad goodbyes, promising to keep in touch on the various projects, literary and conservation-minded, that we have planned for the coming year.

7 / A SEASON
OF CELEBRATIONS

W hen I return from visiting Ted, my thoughts
settle on the Steelhead Society. No longer
president, I feel free to devote myself to the kind of special
projects befitting a past leader. I contact Dan Burns, a young
corporate lawyer, devoted angler and conservationist. I met
Dan at the society's 1992 banquet and auction, one of the
saddest occasions I have ever had to address. Even though
it was a major victory for wild-river conservation with its
gratifying turnout and media coverage, it was sad because
Eugene Rogers had suddenly passed away. It was Eugene
who, after the death of Cal Woods, came to emblematize the
character and quiet determination of the society, especially
during the campaigns to save the Stein River valley and to

halt the Kemano Completion Project. That folly of industrial water diversion would have resulted in an eighty-seven per cent reduction in the flow of the Nechako River.

It was my melancholy duty to eulogize Eugene, a sometimes harsh mentor to me in matters of conservation and public relations. After describing Eugene's unflinching character in taking on conservation projects—but only after careful consideration—and his quiet bulldogged determination, I asked for a moment's silence. Once that moment ended, a tear-streaked Paul George, founder of the more than thirty-thousand-member Western Canada Wilderness Committee, approached the podium. Paul passionately announced the Wilderness Committee would be donating two thousand dollars and establishing an annual Eugene Rogers Conservation Award. It was a fitting tribute to the man and his work, and it energized the room, making the auction the most successful in our history.

Afterwards a slender, handsome, *GQ* sort of fellow in a well-cut pinstriped suit introduced himself and asked whether there was anything he could do to make a contribution. Upon discovering his fertile mind, rife with good ideas, his passion for flyfishing and his joie de vivre, I invited Dan Burns to join the board of the society and we quickly became friends. It is gratifying that he and Ken Kirkby appear compatible working together and that Budge Bell-Irving is especially taken with him, determined to help him and the society in any way he can. Together, Dan and I brainstorm a new scheme: in addition to the annual banquet of the Steelhead Society in late winter, we will organize a much smaller, more expensive evening—black tie optional—that will feature a reading by Ted; in addition, we will present the premiere of *Wild Steelhead of the Skeena*, the film that I have been trying to get off the ground for some time and that is now about to be filmed: a beautiful narrative about the steelhead as a symbol of survival of all things natural and good in the environment. And, finally, an exhibition and sale of Ken Kirkby paintings with half of the proceeds going to the society.

Now we need a motto for the evening, something to tie the elements together. Something to recognize the steelhead as the oldest, most primitive western salmon: the first Pacific variety migrating south into every ecological niche, and the salmon from which the other Pacific varieties descended. Something to tie it to its eastern counterpart, the Atlantic salmon, and finally to the inukshuk, the symbol of man's survival in the frozen Arctic. It occurs to me that Canada's motto *A Mari usque ad Mare* ("From Sea to Sea") tells only part of the story, so I suggest "From Sea to Sea to Sea," which becomes the caption on the limited edition Ken Kirkby print we produce to represent the show and the evening: Symbols of Survival. It is the first time the newly coined phrase appears in print but within a very few years it is being picked up by the politicians.

We approach Budge about the idea and he is keen. Budge and Dan form an indomitable duo, with Budge opening many major corporate and patrons' doors in Vancouver and Dan providing the *coup de grâce:* the pitch. Simon Fraser University's Jack Blaney graciously allows us to use the university's elegant downtown ballroom and, although we have only 180 places at table to sell, we somehow end up selling 210—for a black tie affair in Vancouver in August!

As those plans unfold, I'm experiencing a certain degree of alarm on another front dear to my heart: finding land on the Thompson River. I hear that the twenty-acre property I had planned to buy is doubling in price and so, in addition to my teaching, research and Steelhead Society issues, I begin feverishly looking for something else to buy. Almost instantly, I uncover an adjacent original land grant that the actor Margot Kidder had sold to West Fraser Timber in 1980. West Fraser had planned to use the land for a gravel mine in the twin-tracking project the Canadian National Railway proposed. Thanks to the efforts of Bob Pasco and, to a lesser extent, my own, the court rejected that plan on environmental grounds and West Fraser was stuck with the property. Call it karma, but when I come calling for a piece of it, West Fraser counters that it is happy to sell, but only the complete unit. So, in the spring of '93 Vicky and I become inadvertent land barons, the owners of more than 260 acres of arid meadow and woods and riverbank, the most beautiful and diverse I have ever encountered on the Thompson. When my daughters hear the good news, they decide that the younger, Thea, should marry her fiancé, Sam Anson, there in August. Suddenly, a camp-out, cookout, country-and-western wedding for 150 guests is also being planned.

There is no time to fit in a major steelhead fishing trip, so when Ted arrives for the fundraiser I make arrangements for Joe Saysell, a major and unlikely heroic figure in the environmental struggle, to take us fly-fishing for coho far out at sea. Joe is a native son of Lake Cowichan, a logging community at the source of the Cowichan River and very different from the town of Duncan and the colony of gentlemanly Brits who populate the shores of the river, living in charming country cottages more reminiscent of Wordsworthian England than rough-hewn Vancouver Island. Joe is a wiry, powerful, yet diminutive figure, a great hunter and fisher and close friend of former federal fisheries and environment minister David Anderson. He is a fishing guide and a faller (tree cutter) for a major logging company and he is cut from rough cloth, a true son of the land. Joe cannot abide the duplicity of logging companies that claim they are following an environmentally sustainable regimen. When an Australian TV company showed up asking how things were going, Joe took them to see the brutal destruction of the Nitinat River, with trees dropped into the river, the bank denuded and flood waters scouring the spawning beds. The reaction of his townspeople in Lake Cowichan was remarkable: they shunned him, though he had lived there all his life. It deeply wounded Joe and his wife, Gail, also a native Lake Cowichan resident, but he stuck to his guns. They sustain themselves in isolation by marching to a different, larger drummer: the conservation movement exemplified by the Steelhead Society.

Ted and I take the ferry to Vancouver Island and go to meet Joe at his house. It is a shaded and sequestered sanctuary on the river overseen by huge cedar and fir trees in the area where the steelhead spawn. As we arrive, Joe is organizing the boat trailer we will haul over the top to Nitinat Lake. Joe and Ted have met previously on the Dean River, where Joe spends a month camping in an old, barged-in school bus, his wife's minimum requirement to accompany him into grizzly country.

The trip to the west coast of Vancouver Island is punctuated by a series of rants as Joe rails against the forces of darkness in logging and the corporate world in general, interspersed by spontaneous guffaws to my interjected attempts at wit when he gets too livid and the air in the truck too hot. We arrive at the lake, which is an Indian reserve. The lake empties to the Pacific through a tidal bore–dominated gap that is a death trap unless you know what you are doing. Fortunately for us, Joe does, and we ride the tide out into the open sea and motor over to a cove where Joe has built a primitive hut on a small log boom. It is our luxury fishing lodge for the duration, and it is perfect. Having dropped off crab traps on our way out into the Pacific, we journey over the open sea for about nineteen kilometres without pausing. There, among the anonymous and amorphous swells of the endless Pacific, dogged by the patrols of terns and gulls, Joe cuts the motor and we tie bucktails, large flies with deer hair streaming off them, onto our floating flylines. It is more than a little spooky and seemingly futile as we ride the swells, no shore in sight, our flies surfing along the top. Then we spot something. A squadron of fins: coho in the hundreds, hunting herring and needlefish, attack. It is fast and furious fishing as coho after coho starts strafing our flies. Sometime we have a double going (two rods with fish on at the same time), sometimes a triple. It is perhaps the most frenzied fishing I have ever experienced, and Ted is chortling like a schoolboy.

After a few hours, we head back to the log boom, exhausted from fighting and releasing the coho. Along the way, we pick up our traps, crammed with huge crabs. When we get back to the hut, Joe fires up a large kettle filled with sea water and we boil enough crabs to feed a football team. Once they are ready and the wine has been poured, all that can be heard is the crunching of shell and the sucking of feelers and legs. Crab after crab falls in a primeval scene that would have cost a thousand dollars in a restaurant. But this is better and I can see Ted's eyes glowing in the firelight as finally he rolls onto his side, sips some Sauvignon Blanc and comments: "We are reliving a ten-thousand-year-old ceremony tonight."

"With wine added," I quip.

. . .

WE RETURN TO Pasco Road to a bedlam of ringing phones prompted by last-minute arrangements for the wedding.

Thea and Sam have arrived from Montreal, as has my older daughter Jennifer from England with her husband, Matt, and their baby daughter, Georgia Rose. So life is a swirl of making plans and group dinners: barbecuing and eating on the deck overlooking the eagles and the seals. When the intensity of it all overpowers him, Ted retreats to the little room off the garage that Vicky had dubbed the "stayfree minipad" where he finds respite to write and to rest.

One afternoon, we decide we need a break. Leaving the din behind, Ted and I walk down through the rain-drenched wilderness garden, newly planted with late-blooming rhododendrons and hydrangeas and magnolias in honour of Thea and Sam's impending nuptials. Bushes heavy with blackberries line the path as we pick up the prawn traps and the trolling rods. Delicately beautiful maidenhair ferns, green with blue veins, festoon the cliff where the sun seldom penetrates. Fortunately the tide is high so we are spared the need to carry the rowboat over the treacherous barnacle-covered rocks. A huge fir log, swept in by the tide, booms metronomically in the great cave that gives the area its name: Hole in the Wall. We push off and, with a few swift strokes of the oars, I have us a hundred feet out, and having baited the trap with cat food and fish heads, start to let out the lead-embedded rope. I mark three hundred feet when it goes slack and add another sixty for tidal action—Ted is amazed at the depth. Over the side go the buoys: empty, brightly coloured laundry detergent bottles.

Then we take out our rods for the real fishing. I explain to him that I refuse to leave the dark age of salmon fishing: no cannonball downrigger or depth sounder complicates the process.

Ted retorts: "You are much more forgiving of faulty people than faulty machines. Perhaps that is why you chose to study psychology rather than engineering?"

"I think you're right. But what about you, Ted? Why did you choose poetry, especially poetry about animals living and dying and the cycle of life and death?"

"Like you, I actually chose people, anthropology, because of its study of language and ancient symbols and cultural markers. My son, Nicholas, who can't walk past a puddle without wondering if there are fish in it, by contrast, prefers animals to people, and so chose biology. But poetry chose me. I did not choose to write poetry. I have to. And when I don't or go off the rails—for example, when I write prose like the *Shakespeare and the Goddess* work—it is almost always a bad decision and I suffer both physically and spiritually. But that one I just had to get off my chest, though it almost killed me."

Nothing left to do then but to let out our trolling lines. After a few minutes even my feverish mind starts to slow and we watch the eagles wheeling in the now clearing deep blue sky and our naval escort: a curious seal that follows us hopefully at about fifty feet.

"Strike!" Ted's rod bends sharply and the Daiwa reel whirs. He is fast to a salmon and, at this time of year in that location, a big salmon is a very big chinook. Ted's eyes light up as he fights the fish, slowing its run by palming the reel. Finally he announces: "It's starting to come in!" And he begins to gain on it. Suddenly there is a tremendous pull, then slack. A few seconds later, a crash on the surface. The seal has wrenched his salmon off the line and is now chasing it, as it was too large to subdue with a single bite. Then all is quiet. Not a ripple on the surface. Who won? Within a minute the seal appears on the surface, alone. The salmon has escaped, but certainly not unscathed.

We console ourselves by hauling up the traps, an arduous task but an insight into why commercial fishermen are so passionate about their work. You never know what bounty lies in store. This time it is a bonanza: dozens of huge, orange spotted prawns, enough to feed the multitude assembled in the house on the cliff. We arrive at the jetty to find Mark Hume, a senior *Vancouver Sun* journalist, waiting for us. There is the usual testosterone rush prompted by being the successful hunter (or, in this case, gatherer). Mark has been incredibly conscientious and influential in covering fisheries conservation issues and the workings of the Steelhead Society. He's here to do a short interview with Ted promoting the Symbols of Survival banquet. They get on well as Ted describes the importance of wild fish and what steelhead have come to mean to him. Ted, feeling he has taken a risk by granting the first interview in many years, is pleased when it is published the next day, focusing mostly on his interest in conservation with only an oblique reference to his marriage to Sylvia, which too often overwhelms any coverage he gets in the media in North America.

On the day of the banquet, Ted spends a great deal of time in the minipad preparing his reading and forming his thoughts. I am in a frenzy answering the phone about the banquet and the sale of the paintings, but also about the arrival of wedding guests and the actual wedding meal itself—the original organizer has bowed out and a former whitewater rafting outfitter who knows how to feed many people in the wilderness has gamely taken on the organization of the wedding, but a hundred decisions must still be made.

And suddenly we are in our finery and arrive at Simon Fraser University at the stroke of six o'clock. The reception room is already full and the boxes of Ted's books of poetry have sold out. Tanned dinner-jacketed individuals wait to have their copies inscribed. The ballroom where the dinner is to be held is a sea of flowers and candles and china, much more festive than I had dared hope for. The last-minute volunteers, including Thea and her maid of honour, Shannon Densmore, have done well in arranging the flowers and dealing with the myriad other details that arise during such occasions.

Having welcomed everyone and proposed a toast to the queen, I introduce Dan, who says a few words about the society and then introduces John Fraser, Speaker of the House of Commons and a founding member of the Steelhead Society. John, in turn, introduces Ted, quoting a critic who called him the "most important poet writing in English in the latter half of the twentieth century."

Ted rises in his white dinner jacket and begins his presentation. He enthralls with his recitation of growing up in the Pennines, of his father returning from the war a damaged man, of his mother's death, of being a child and seeing a flight of bombers pass overhead, of the October salmon in its spawning colours, of the river in low water and perhaps most poignantly for the B.C. crowd: "The Bear," the story of our first steelhead trip to the Dean told in verse. I am touched and very amused when he dedicates a poem to me: "Don't Answer the Phone," a characterization of our hectic past week; and even more so when he dedicates a reading of a poem to Sam and Thea who are sitting in the audience: "Bride and Groom Lie Hidden for Three Days."

The audience loves the intimacy and elegance of the setting. It turns out to be the most successful evening ever for the Steelhead Society—financially, socially and politically.

The next day Ted takes it easy as panic over the approaching wedding mounts all around him. He appears for a leisurely breakfast of smoked salmon omelette with espresso and multigrain toast, then retreats to the minipad to write. His only duty is a visit to CBC Radio, where he is interviewed on the breakfast show. Rather than reading one of his own poems, he gives a rendition of the ancient Irish classic *"Donal Og"* ("Young Donald"). The radio silence following his deep resonant voice is palpable.

We organize a first birthday party for my granddaughter, Georgia Rose, and Ted writes a poem that is mounted on a rocket and shot off onto the ocean. No copy survives today, unless good fortune still protects the original on the ocean floor. Six-year-old Alexei and his friend Christian are solic- itous serving as Georgia's attendants and she takes it all in stride, chocolate cake smearing her cherubic visage. Among the ice cream and (soft) drinks, the bells and balloons and ribbons that festoon the house, Ted, sitting in his suit, gath- ering his thoughts, watches her with an affectionate, con- tented smile.

.   .   .

THAT NIGHT WE attend Ted's second reading at Simon Fraser University's Harbour Centre. The venue is a far cry from the cavernous immensity of UBC's Recital Hall where I first met him. It is in a well-appointed executive-MBA-type lecture hall that holds no more than a hundred and sadly, given the short notice, is not filled, but the crowd is very intense and attentive. Ted gives the same intimate reading he always does but in the subdued light of the room, with much more a sense of dialogue than monologue, and the audience, serious students and fans of his poetry, is once again capti- vated. Having just spent a couple of weeks with him, I never- theless want the reading to go on and on.

And once again, he is infinitely patient after the reading, meeting with admirers and, especially, writers. One who stands out is Sandra Lockwood, an exotic looking and very talented performance poet, songwriter and singer who has attracted a lot of attention in the local media, most prominently for appearing on stage with only a fresh salmon bound to her breast in a performance she calls *River*. She shows Ted a bundle of her poems and then suddenly bolts, pausing once she has overcome her anxiety to chat with me at the door and divulge how his writing has struck a chord with her like no one else's. I am mildly surprised, given her public image as an experimental writer and performer who is very hip and controversial, her persona and her work, which at first bluff are very unlike the traditional poetry that Ted appears to represent.

Later, I shall read some of her work and realize it is much more influenced by Ted's than I would ever have predicted. Ted, too, is impressed by her writing and so later I relate to him that she is controversial for wearing the salmon, even having been condemned by some puerile activists as engaging in "bestiality." It is the most outlandish stretch of political correctness I have ever encountered. Nevertheless, Sandra was apparently very wounded by the accusation, especially since it occurred during the Women in View Festival, where the official line is supposed to be one of mutual support. I also relate to him an interview she gave wherein she revealed that she suffers from a psychosis that led to her starring in a medical training film for the University of Toronto. That, in turn, leads to a discussion about the thin line that sometimes separates genius from madness, a common theme in the psychoanalysis of literature and art, and one that Ken and I have explored many times. Not one that has afflicted Ted's own family but certainly relevant to his relationship with Sylvia, a topic we will eventually discuss in great detail.

After the reading, we are off on a tour of local bars in honour of Sam Anson's impending marriage to Thea. She and her female friends have left on their own version of the tour with the plan that we shall rendezvous at the end of the evening at Bar None, a popular nightspot owned in part by Greg Belzberg, one of Dan's friends. Ted suggests he is too tired to come along, but we insist, pointing out that given the distance to our house near Horseshoe Bay, he is a captive until the end of the evening.

It is 1993. The Drake is one of the pre-eminent strip bars in Vancouver—nicely appointed with mahogany bar counters, brass railings, dance poles and hardwood ramps; its luxurious plush semicircular booths and leather bar stools bely its location in the gritty downtown eastside. The stage is central, with arms going off in two directions: brass poles that the dancers swing on are located at each extremity. In two corners there are small stages with poles for the moments when all the dancers perform simultaneously or for semiprivate dances for the patrons who wish to pay extra. The background is very dark but the stage lights are a veritable kaleidoscope of colour and the sound system is of extremely high quality. It is usually played at a deafening volume that obviates the need for conversation either among those sitting discreetly at the tables some distance from the action or

in the single seats lining the arms dubbed "gynecology row"
—intended for those spectators fascinated by the intimate
details of the female anatomy. We choose one of the more
discreet tables and at that moment the whole ensemble is on
stage, so one can admire the spectrum of female pulchritude
performing that night.

"Who are the patrons?" asks Ted.

"Everyone in Vancouver: stockbrokers, loggers, students,
businessmen and workers, even the occasional academic,
though probably not many priests in full regalia—like most
of Vancouver, it is confusing to the visitor and very demo-
cratic: for the price of a beer, a lonely fellow who otherwise
may never have the opportunity can see a beautiful woman
dance naked a few feet away. And unlike the treatment of
male strippers by women patrons, they are treated with rev-
erence—there is also a 'no touch' policy."

"What about the women dancing? Who are they? Are
they well paid?"

"Aspiring actresses and dancers, students, often women
who would otherwise have low-paying waitress jobs but
make good incomes because they have a valuable resource—
their beauty and ability to move gracefully—to trade on for
a limited number of years, probably ten or fifteen max, if they
are in good shape and take care of themselves. Look at that
beautiful woman spinning on that pole—like a professional
athlete but with a career that is longer than a model's, given
the obsession in that business with ingénues."

"How do they get a job?"

"I don't know, but I do know there is a local professional school that trains aspiring strippers and there is a hierarchy of venues, from seedy bars in the Interior to the most prestigious in Vancouver and Victoria."

"They are so much more elegant and feminine than I recall from my youth in England, in the army, where the setting was not so prepossessing and the women so lissome and elegant. Nor did they remove all their clothes. Amazing."

Dan, who does not favour the Drake as a drinking establishment but has agreed to come on the tour, leans over as an especially graceful beauty with honey blonde hair to her waist, long legs and perfect breasts walks off the stage naked, gathering up her costume: "What do you say, Ted? Are those hatchery or wild?"

Ted laughs. "At this distance they definitely appear to be a gift of Mother Nature rather than products of the cosmetic surgeon's art."

"Let's find out," says Dan and approaches her to ask how much she would charge for a dance for just our little gang, in honour of the budding bridegroom. The deal completed, she mounts our ministage and somehow maintains the innocence and demureness of a schoolgirl while treating Sam and the rest of us to an especially lovely rendition of the ecdysiast's art, swirling and smiling and stretching on the pole and the stage for the length of, "Nights in White Satin," a classic song that dates from the high school proms of my youth. For a brief moment we are all transported to a more innocent time. Coming back to earth we applaud and rise to leave in order to join the women's tour at Bar None.

Bar None's popularity renders its name ironic, for as we approach the club in Yaletown, the lineup of hopeful patrons winds around the block. Dan had suggested we go in the backdoor to avoid any acrimony and has gone ahead. After parking my truck, I lead a dubious Ted around to the back. The idea of taking the Poet Laureate on a tour of Vancouver nightspots appeals to my sense of the incongruous— some would say the perverse. I believe acquaintanceship and especially friendship should promote exposure to people and activity that would not occur during one's regular routine. And this is certainly not Ted's, though he wears a smile beneath his furrowed brow.

At the back door there is also a group of people waiting to get in, obviously second tier on the guest list, but I spot Dan disappearing through the door, so I burst into a sprint. Too late. He is gone as I arrive and a disgruntled bouncer will have none of us, pushing Ted and me back among the wannabes as we try to follow even as I explain my connection to the owner. He eyes me as if I were a maggot on a chop, clearly disbelieving that anyone of my advanced age and "clear-cut" pate would have privileged entry into his *über-cool* workplace. I am not inclined to argue, and Ted urges that we head for Pasco Road.

Just as we turn to go, Dan darkens the doorway and shouts: "Ehor, Ted, this way. What happened?" I explain our lack of the right stuff at which point an infuriated Dan lets us in and, with Greg standing by, insists that the bouncer not only apologize but get down on his knees to do so. Although I find all of this faintly amusing, Ted is much chagrined and ready to bolt, so I insist only on a handshake and an oral expression of regret from our now thoroughly chastened former nemesis, who despite Dan's colourful descriptions of our credentials is clearly no follower of academe or the arts.

As we enter the main floor, a blast of sound greets our ears and there, on one side of the dance floor, are Thea and her gang, with Jennifer just departing to relieve the babysitter, all laughing and chatting and sipping drinks. Thea is much more voluble than usual, of course feeling some responsibility to be the life of the party. After we greet everyone and have one drink Ted and I depart, leaving the younger members to move on to Greg's apartment for the denouement to the evening. Ted's flight home the next day calls for an early night. The bouncer is especially gracious and polite to us as we exit.

· · ·

ONE HUNDRED AND fifty guests from Canada, the United States and Europe head up Highway 1 into the desert. The ceremony is conducted under an arbour of wildflowers, with vows exchanged by the river under an evening sky streaked with pastels of gold and pink. The highlight of the ceremony is a reading of Ted's poem "Bride and Groom" by two of Thea and Sam's friends. It's like an echo of Ted himself is caught here. Thea is radiant-looking, with her dark eyes, black hair and deeply tanned complexion—perfectly at ease in whatever environment she finds herself. Accompanied on guitar by John Forrest, a virtuoso jazz musician, I sing a Ukrainian love song, *"Zhow be ya banduru"* ("I take up my guitar"), that my father used to sing to my mother. The wedding is wonderful. Only one guest runs into a rattlesnake, with no loss of life or limb. When the wedding couple retire to their tent, they are startled to discover mysterious amulets strung from it, including a dead snake. They take them for a good sign.

We, the hangers-on, raise a toast by the campfire to our friend Ted, and I recall how, as we drove to the airport, Ted was ebullient: he commented repeatedly about how rich the visit had been and how he would export the energy we have generated in British Columbia on behalf of conservation to England to try to address the major issues confronting the West Country and other rivers: pollution from farm runoff of fertilizers and silage (which will eventually be identified as the culprit in bovine spongiform encephalopathy leading to many cases of horrific Creutzfeldt-Jakob disease in humans in the U.K.) and of course rampant slaughter by gillnetters in the estuaries. When I dropped him off he grasped me in a powerful bear hug far beyond the ritualized tense embrace customary of males. As I struggled to catch my breath, he said: "You've done so much this year, but now you have to concentrate on saving your own life. That little room you call the minipad that I used must be your sanctuary, just as my writing hut is for me: no telephone, TV, family or marriage issues. Just you and a piece of paper. Do it!"

8 / DEATH AND RENEWAL

As 1994 dawns, my marriage appears to be withering in a melancholy though civil way. I spend a great deal of time with my son but it is not enough to fill the void. I consult with my friends and all of them underline what Barry Stuart advises: "Stop obsessing and take on a major project, something you can bury yourself in and be proud of." Finally John Hamill says: "Ehor, as I tell my children, there are people in this world who are determined to be happy and others who are determined not to be. You have always been one of those determined to be happy, so stop moping and get on with it."

On the heels of that sage wisdom, a very long, typewritten letter arrives from Ted, and though he comments that there is little of note to report, he immediately betrays parental concern over the fact he hasn't heard from Nick since before Christmas, doesn't know where he is or how to get in touch with him. As Ted had mentioned to me and Nick had elaborated upon, Nick likes to head down to Belize to fish for tarpon in the winter, sometimes alone, sometimes with female companionship. We never stop being parents, I ponder, as I look at six-year-old Alexei beavering away on a drawing of an airplane at the kitchen counter. Some things never change.

As is his wont, Ted describes the state of the rivers—at the moment in terrible flood and, consequently, the salmon redds, nests full of fertilized eggs, may be washed out. Fishing is like farming: either too little or too much rain is the chronic state of affairs; only occasionally are we graced with the optimal amount, and then one worries about the size of the returning run of salmon or steelhead and whether they have survived the perils of their five- to nearly ten-thousand-kilometre odyssey. I can hear him sighing as he says that, at his age, he is trying to do what he should have done yesterday, like the beauty queen as she plucks grey hairs out of her nostrils. He vows to write a book about what the older generation failed to warn us. But then he veers to fishing again, saying he got a wonderful photo from Jay holding a beautiful Dean River steelhead and sporting an elastic band smile. And wonders when he can join us once again on that fabled river.

He has enclosed a couple of copies of *The Iron Woman*, the distaff version of *The Iron Man*, his popular children's book, and laments that Pete Townshend, who had written some good sounds for the musical play version of *The Iron Man*, had misled people into thinking it would be a challenge to the Cameron Mackintosh extravaganzas; in reality, it was a fine though modest children's Christmas workshop, even though it had an amazing twenty-foot iron man as the centrepiece.

Ted reveals he has cancelled some fishing on the Connon because last year vanished before his eyes and he must get through what he started. He says he is writing away to get himself into something worthwhile, simultaneously taking a strip out of himself for having been diverted into the Shakespeare book and some collections of other prose work he produced over the years. Now he is struggling to centre himself in his more natural creative element, presumably poetry, while the negative after-effects of his diversion into prose keep trying to undermine his efforts.

He ends by decrying the English child's lack of genuine, unfiltered experience in the real, the natural world, suggesting that video games are a Japanese plot and that I should accidentally step on Alexei's, if he has one, to save him from that electronic prison of modern-day Casper Hausers. I know it is to purge the depression he experiences thinking of thousands of children locked in virtual, sterile reality that he ends the missive by penning in the exciting news that there is incontrovertible evidence now that big cats—black panthers and so on—are living in the wild in England and even interbreeding with Scottish wildcats. For Ted, the panacea to the downward spiral produced by technological, sensory analgesia is discovering a new mystery in nature.

I write back to reassure Ted that I am determined to offer Alexei alternatives to the sterile electronic universe, to give him a world he will find so compelling that he will seek it out—a more rewarding mysterious reality—for solace. I tell Ted that I awoke one golden Sunday morning when the migrating birds were rioting in the garden to find a yellow sticky note on the kitchen counter: "We're in the forest playing Love Alexei xox 8:45." Coming in for lunch three hours later with his buddy Christian, he informed me that while they were playing in their "base" a mountain lion had obliviously slunk past them. I carry that note in my address book to this day.

Then an opportunity arrives that is beyond expectation. Gary Anderson, who is a close friend and professor at McGill University, has become involved in setting up Atlantic salmon fishing camps on the Kola Peninsula, the same area Michael Heathcoat Amory and his friends caught 190 salmon. Until the fall of the Soviet Union it was an impermeable Arctic fortress east of Scandinavia, sheltering cruise missile silos and nuclear submarine bases. All the settlers in the area had been ejected or killed off by the Communists after the revolution, so the ironic upside is that the rivers there are pristine, untouched by pollution or the mixed blandishments of humanity. They harbour the greatest intact runs of large Atlantic salmon left in the world, in true wilderness settings.

Given my experience on the West Coast with steelhead, Gary asks whether I would like to assemble a group
of expert fishers and managers to serve as coordinators at
camps on the Varzuga and Varzina rivers the next summer.
Not employment but adventure is the offer. It is the kind of
escape and wilderness psychotherapy I need. I accept immediately. I broach the subject with Ted but he still has no interest in visiting Russia. My friends Dan Burns, John Hamill
and Jay Rowland and a fourth, a talented though somewhat
irascible aboriginal fisher, fly tier and artist named Joe Kambeitz, are all eager for the adventure, however. It proves to be
one of my life's most exciting escapades.

Coming back through London in July, I call Ted and we
agree to meet in Soho. He is looking fit and tanned and eager
to hear of my adventures running a giant Mikoyan 8 helicopter loaded with clients over the Kola Peninsula as vast waves
of reindeer form a living sea on the Russian tundra below. I
describe how we end up using KGB border guards armed with
AK-47s to drive off competing Finnish fishing interlopers who
do not have the permits we do but have paid off somebody
in the bureaucracy to poach our waters. The country is vast,
desolate and painfully beautiful, with powerful rivers pouring out of the highlands through rocky canyons. And the fish
are big, silver torpedoes that can wreck your tackle if they get
past the midnight poaching vessels parked in the estuaries.

We head to my daughter Jennifer's flat in Putney Bridge,
where we sit sipping my duty-free Scotch—Highland Park

from the distant Orkneys, an outpost that I imagine could pass for Russia—and it doesn't disappoint: slightly smoky but heathery and delicate, like the tiny twisting, graceful birches of the Russian tundra that Dan called lovely young ballerinas.

Rising at half past seven we head for Devon on a day that turns out to be the hottest in a hundred years. Carol greets me warmly at Court Green and I meet Ted's Aunt Hilda, who at eighty-five is very lively and delightful company, obviously proud of her nephew. I very much enjoy her stories of the family, which inspires Ted to haul out a shoebox of photos, and accompanying the dog-eared, browned snapshots I get thumbnail sketches of his kindly wise mother, his taciturn father, who was so wounded emotionally by the war but would never speak of it, and his larger-than-life brother, Gerald. But most of all, stories of Olwyn, his glamorous, vivacious older sister and literary agent who kept his head above water during his dark days and, of course, unintentionally set the scene for his falling in love with Carol.

The next day we drive over to the farm of Michael and Clare Morpurgo, people whom Ted admires deeply. Michael is not there but Clare, an ebullient, rosy-cheeked, raven-haired woman, greets us and we chat amiably for awhile and then say our goodbyes. On the way to Court Green Ted fills me in on how Michael, a teacher and writer of children's books, decided along with Clare years before to do something about the paucity of life experience of inner city children and so established Farms for City Children, a charity that takes kids from the city and puts them to work on real farms, hoping to enrich their understanding of how the world actually works. I understand more clearly now the concerns Ted voiced in his letter about children living like Casper Hausers in their electronic cages of TV and video games. Apparently Farms for City Children has been an amazing success and now operates three farms. "I really respect people who do something on their own, not waiting for government or someone else," he says wistfully, then sighs and changes the subject. He seems strangely melancholy. The next day Ted drops me off at the station. Bad timing. The office of Poet Laureate confers upon Ted the princely sum of a hundred pounds sterling per year and a butt of dry sack wine from the Sherry Institute of Spain, an allotment that he had worked to reinstitute. It was to arrive that day.

· · ·

TED PHONES IN early January 1995 to announce he has "dug himself out of his quagmire" and is ready to return to the Dean. I am elated and we make plans to take the final week of August, as we usually do when it is available, a dodgy time for weather but also less crowded and sometimes rewarded with a late raft of giant fish arriving with the first rains of autumn. It is a much quieter time on Pasco Road than the previous summer, and Ted and I spend the days in leisurely preparation for the trip, heading to Granville Island, an urban market in downtown Vancouver, for specialty items and for our traditional, first-evening-on-the-Dean seafood feast.

On the penultimate evening we host a dinner. To the dinner I invite Tom Pero, editor of *Wild Steelhead and Salmon,* a fine angling and conservation magazine based in Bellevue, Washington, and various friends—anglers of all sizes and stripes, and conservationists who have helped us in our wild river campaigns and who might appreciate meeting a poet and, in my opinion, philosopher of wilderness in the tradition of Rousseau and Thoreau. Tom appears a little distracted, perhaps overwhelmed by the occasion and the gathering of so many luminaries, British, American and Canadian, in conservation and writing. He is very excited to meet Ted, and that he has agreed to be interviewed, having acceded on so few occasions. The sun is drumming down on the deck, the Pacific a glistening azure mirror as Tom, Ted and I seat ourselves around the table, in hand glasses of fine Pinot Gris, my favourite B.C. wine, one that can stand up to varietals from anywhere. For a few moments we are content merely to watch the eagles dive-bomb the family of swimming mergansers that not long ago left its nest in the hollow snag looming over the sea cave.

Ted starts to reflect on salmon fishing in England. He relates how "because of the traditional background of salmon sport fishing by the rich and upper middle class, preserved for them rather like grouse shooting and pheasant shooting, the antagonism between the nets men, who were just the local boys down in the estuary, and the owners of the sport fishery became a social war, a class war. And that has absolutely bedevilled it. It's almost impossible for the two groups to talk together as we would, about their common interest in protecting the same stock of fish." He stops and stares out at the eagle perched in the top of the great Douglas fir above the sea cave.

Ted looks very handsome, tanned and robust but I notice his hair backlit by the sun is now almost snowy white. Later that evening I point out we have the same animosities here in British Columbia. Gillnetters wipe out stocks of rare and extremely valuable steelhead in their pursuit of sockeye for commercial gain or, even more sadly, in their pursuit of pink or chum salmon of very little market value and often only to qualify for unemployment benefits. When you dig deep enough you discover they just love their lifestyle: getting out on their boat and competing with one another, which is why they don't want to use estuary traps and weirs that would allow the corralling of target species and the release of threatened stocks and game fish like steelhead and coho. And would not require their expensive boats whose cost they constantly bewail.

We talk about the importance of fishing, and Ted agrees that: "If ever they abolish fishing, I would have to leave the country. I'd have to go live in a land where I can still keep hold of the world . . . To lose that would be like learning to live without kidneys. You'd have to live with a biology you'd diminished. You'd live an artificially diminished life. If I were deprived of that kind of live, intimate, interactive

existence—allowing myself to be possessed by and possess-
ing this sort of world through fishing, through that whole
corridor back into the world that made us as we are, turned
us into what we are—it would be as though I had some great,
vital part of me amputated."

Ted is deeply wound up now. Beads of sweat glisten on
his forehead and his eyes squint as if to penetrate the oceanic
meniscus shimmering far below, where now a ripple reveals
a ling cod rising to take a small fish. The eagle, its fiery eye
fixed on the centre of the radiating rings, shifts its weight on
its perch, flexes its feathers but makes no further move.

Tom asks: "You think we'd be a less healthy society if we
gave up hunting and fishing?"

"Very much so. Yes. And less wise, less sensitive to the
whole picture or the consequences of our activity on the
environment. You're not only going fishing, you're going
on some sort of reconnection with the most valuable things
in yourself. The unspoiled. That feeling of something absolutely sacred and unspoiled is a big part of that, isn't it? That's
what you are looking for. You want to be reconnected with
that . . . hoping to get it back, to make it part of yourself, to
repossess it . . .

"Any kind of fishing provides that connection with the
whole living world. It gives you the opportunity of being
totally immersed, turning back into yourself in a good way.
A form of meditation. Some form of communion with levels
of yourself that are deeper than the ordinary self. When I am

fishing alone, as I come out of it, if I have to speak to somebody, I find I can't speak properly. I can't form words. The words sort of come out backwards, tumbled. It takes time to readjust, as if I'd been into some part of myself that predates language."

Of course! I exclaim to myself. Then out loud: "People and problems in our lives have become so complex and overwhelming, fishing can provide sanctuary. Rivers can become a place of escape, hidden little sanctuaries. You come back to the everyday world and you realize these problems maybe aren't that important after all. You're diminished in a good way."

"That's why," Ted continues, "it's so perversely painful and horrible when one of these wild places is polluted and spoiled. When that pure source is poisoned, to me that is the ultimate kind of atrocity—a vandalism against the most essential thing in us, an act of violence against mankind."

After Sylvia died, he says, he went to live in Ireland. "By then I'd already begun to be pretty interested in salmon. I used to poach the odd one, in Devon. The night before I left for Ireland, I was walking beside a little stream on Dartmoor . . . And this stream went over a cliff. I went down the cliff where the falling water joined a big, swift river . . . And coming up this river were these big salmon. As they came past me they were leaping. And as they leapt they shook themselves in the air. As they shook themselves in the air their milt and spawn were splashed over me. I was completely covered in milt and spawn from these leaping salmon . . . these giant salmon as they went past. Since that dream, all my recurrent fish dreams have been about salmon."

The frail cry of the eagle pierces the tranquility of the sun-drenched afternoon as it finally swoops from the tree and takes a small merganser. Ted watches the eagle creak away with its prize, then at Tom's request begins to read a favourite poem, "October Salmon," and its hero resting "in that lap of easy current / In his graveyard pool."

·   ·   ·

OUR LAST TRIP together into the Dean is especially exhilarating. A bright day attended by the usual patrol of mountain goats gazing at us bemusedly from impossibly small ledges overhanging thousand-foot cliffs and the river, a cobalt ribbon, low and bright and clear as we chopper into a campsite even more elegant than last year. Now netting overlays the brightly coloured tarps to quell gale-force winds and the stove, after so many years of my lobbying, is finally a propane model that may alleviate the occupational hazard of the naphtha burner's flaring up and setting the tarps alight, which has happened on more than one occasion. The outgoing group is in high spirits, having hooked 105 steelhead, landing forty-nine, one of the most productive sojourns ever.

Ted, Dan and Jay distribute themselves in the pools around camp. They have filled the likely spots, so on a hunch I head downstream on my own to Victoria. I can't believe my

good fortune: no one is around, the stories of endless numbers of Italians from Nakia Lodge and other campers obviously a bad news hyperbole. I have a strange sense of reprise:
on my second trip to the Dean I decided to fish the dry fly
exclusively despite its lesser chance of producing a hookup,
rather than going to the old reliable of a deeply sunken fly for
at least first blood. I tie on a No. 1—sized Thompson River
Rat of spun white caribou and chartreuse hackle, wing and
tail. Spey cast (a figure-eight mode of hurtling out the fly not
requiring a backcast), my fly lands in Victoria's throat. The
fly skitters around unmolested. But was that a slight bulge
behind it as it turned the corner? Rather than lengthening
the line, I pause for thirty seconds, recheck my knot, pulling
the loops tight, and then cast again. And again a bulge, this
time accompanied by a bow wave that sends the fly through
the air. But no cigar.

My hand is trembling as I regroup, look at the mighty
chief—the cliff opposite me where the waterfall is barely
a trickle—then cast again. A mighty fish comes out of the
water, head and shoulders to the sun, and engulfs the fly on
the way back down. It is a savage attack. I am fast to a loco-
motive that thunders downstream in a series of porpoising
leaps, and very soon I am in pursuit, my backing line down to
the last few turns. Then it rockets upstream, my line forming
a huge circle as I wind to catch up. I never do. The fly comes
back to me, slightly tatty but still serviceable. Three more
fish track my fly, chase it, whack it, but are never hooked as I

am left a nervous wreck over the next hour. Perhaps I should have relented and put on a wet fly, but so long as the water remains clear, this will be a dry-fly trip. Then it is time to head back to hear the stories and share mine.

Dan and Jay are busy preparing supper when I get to the camp pool. Ted is sitting and watching the river, pen and paper in hand, so I pause at the new seam in the current on the camp side, a likely spot for a steelhead to be lying. I can't resist taking a cast and on my third I am fast to a wild eleven-pound hen, as my gallery cheers me on. I manage to beach her without a downstream pursuit, which is a good thing as the logjam is impassable.

One cool night that week, the sky ablaze with stars, we have just had an elaborate meal of spiced beef, wild rice and steamed vegetables topped with two bottles of fine California Cabernet Sauvignon. We watch a very large grizzly, in his hunt for maggots, toss aside a tree trunk like a piece of kindling. We are sipping Irish coffees as Ted takes it all in with a contented smile. Then Dan tells a wild story of his adventures in China and Thailand. He asks Ted whether he has experienced anything comparable.

"It would be the time I spent with Peter Brook and his troupe touring through Persia. But the wilder adventure occurred in Africa where they often stopped to perform in small villages in the jungle"—this was a tour that apparently he did not actually accompany them upon, as I discovered upon reading Brook's *The Conference of the Birds*, though

Ted's retelling was so animated, it seemed like he had been there. "There were many actors, including Helen Mirren, and I had created a language for the production based on onomatopoeia that was intended to be universal. In one village they were performing in the square with the king seated on a throne-type seat and a fire in the centre and the villagers gathered round by the hundreds. An actor who was intended to be an evil spirit came out wearing a hideous mask and stalked around trying to intimidate the audience. He came up to the king and shouted"—here Ted strings together a sequence of vowels and consonants—"hoping to frighten them. It was supposed to mean 'deep, black terrifying hole leading to hell.' They did look a little startled so he shouted even louder in the king's and his court's faces . . . and then a titter swept through the crowd that rose to a crescendo as the actor shouted louder and louder in desperation. People were rolling on the ground laughing hysterically. Finally the spirit slunk off the stage, completely cowed. When Peter asked the king through an interpreter what had happened, he explained, still chuckling, that the actor had kept shouting, 'big, black hairy cunt' in their language."

After recovering from my startled outburst of guffaws, I realize it is the only time, barring Jay's fortieth birthday poem, over all those years that I have heard Ted utter a crude word, or even a curse—an amazing record in company that is known occasionally to fall from grace in its use of language—and even then he is merely quoting, and even by the poetic standard he enunciated in *Poetry in the Making*, the usage is eminently apropos.

When the others go off to bed, Ted and I stay a little while chatting. I ask him again about Sylvia and the poems he has written about her. This time he says he feels it is time to publish them. I ask why but he does not answer directly. He pauses and appears for a moment to be deeply lost in thought, a world away from me, this fire, the river. Finally, he offers in a soft rumbling tone: "The time is right to get them off my chest. And there are so many of them."

We sit in silence for a long time.

"You know, Ehor, you have done so much for me. Opened up doors and experiences that have been closed for years. In some ways, though your interests are different, you remind me a great deal of my brother. I hope, in some small way, I have done something for you."

I am stunned: a thousand answers run through my mind. Can he not see how much he enriches my life, the lives of everyone he touches in Vancouver as he does in England? But I only say: "Ted, you are like the brother I never had, and for that I thank you." It is the last time we see each other.

. . .

OVER THE NEXT two years, with both Ted's life and my own in disarray, we do not visit but speak occasionally over the phone, making plans. I hear rumours that Ted is ill but he is vague on the subject. Then, in the spring of 1998, Nick phones to tell me that Ted is quite depressed about his illness. Apparently it is serious and Nick suggests that I phone. When I do, Ted and I have a long chat and, thankfully, I make him laugh and offer to visit but, after reflecting on my offer, he puts me off, suggesting that I wait, that like an old bear he is in his cave healing himself. He says much the same thing when I phone in the fall to congratulate him on his being appointed to the queen's Order of Merit. I should have gone.

I get the call from my son-in-law Sam on a shimmering sunny day in October 1998. He heard the bad news on KCRW, the NPR station Thea works for in Santa Monica. As I hang up the phone, a sensation comes over me that I am being smothered in layers of heavy felt, one after another landing on me, weighing me down, suffocating me until I can no longer stand. Their pungent, damp odour is overpowering. I drag myself outside onto the deck and flop into a chair. A snow-white ferry glides silently by.

I cannot get to the family funeral in North Tawton, but his old friend Seamus Heaney does and he says what we all might say:

No death outside my immediate family has left me feeling more bereft. No death in my lifetime has hurt poets more. He was a tower of tenderness and strength, a great arch under which the least of poetry's children could enter and feel secure. His creative powers were, as Shakespeare said, still crescent. By his death the veil of poetry is rent, and the walls of learning broken.

Ted on the Dock at Nitinat, Vanisle

ACKNOWLEDGEMENTS

This book is the brainchild of Scott Steedman, former associate publisher at Douglas & McIntyre. Scott, although originally a biologist, is a worldly man of diverse interests who was in the audience at the reading given by Ted Hughes at the University of British Columbia (but sadly enough never met him). Scott and I did not actually meet until 2003, when he and his wife, Leilah Nadir—now an accomplished writer—generously offered to work as caterers on *Riverburn,* the film my daughters Thea and Jennifer were making on our property, Nighthawk Ranch, on the Thompson River. Even then, he and I did not really get to know each other until I hosted his bachelor party at Nighthawk a few years ago. After all the festivities Scott and his friends and I partook in that weekend, I am gratified that he still had the confidence in my abilities to produce this manuscript.

Although I had already written some short pieces about Ted, given the sometimes dubious industry that had sprung up around his work and life, I was extremely ambivalent about writing this book about a good, kind man, our experiences together and his extraordinary vision of the world. Once written, it seemed doomed to moulder in manuscript. But after a couple of false starts, Scott announced he'd found an editor appropriate for the task. I had concerns that we needed a person, rare in literary circles, attuned to the unusual spirit of the material: an ethos embracing both physical wilderness adventure and a specific poetic and interpersonal world view. The editor's suggestions would not only burnish the prose and heighten the excitement of the expeditions, but lead to structural alterations and, alas, sometimes ruthlessly excise the dross. I am relieved that John Burns, despite not coming from the literary tradition of the outdoors nor being an angler, proved to be everything I had hoped for in an editor, and I am grateful for his skillful efforts.

. . .

I THANK Ann-Marie Metten for her assiduously conscientious copy editing of the manuscript. Perusing her documentation was like taking a course in fact checking and has made me a more careful researcher.

. . .

I CONSULTED MY daughters, and Jennifer, ever the optimist and supporter, was immensely enthusiastic. That in turn bolstered my determination to do it. Thea was more hesitant, not only having spent a great deal more time with Ted and me, but wondering, being a very private person, whether some things should not remain unwritten; an unusually sensitive perspective on the part of a young woman who is herself a writer. Fortunately her support for the project rose dramatically when she read the early chapters. After some reflection, I began to believe I was on the right track. The careful reading and insightful comments of her husband, Sam Anson, also a writer, added immeasurably to my production in those wobbly early days. Those reassurances were underscored by the reaction of my son, Alexei, a passionate angler and nascent writer himself, who declared after reading a couple of chapters on the steelhead fishing expeditions, that whatever other value the book had, the record of those fabled trips alone was important to commit to print. Together, their views tipped the balance.

I owe a great deal to the camaraderie of my friends who so enriched the times we spent together with Ted: John Hamill, ever the adventurer, full of passion and spontaneity and good fellowship; Dan Burns whose (to us) amusing foibles and misadventures transformed into grace under fire and unyielding strength and loyalty in all situations; Jay Rowland, whose wry, slightly jaded view of the world kept us honest and organized; and Ken Kirkby, the best of company, who in the gloomiest times led by example and reminded me that the conservation struggle, regardless of public reaction, was its own reward. I also have to thank Barry Stuart, who did not spend as much time with Ted as the others, but was there for me when I needed him most. We all owe a debt of gratitude to the Totem Flyfishers of British Columbia, who in their quiet, modest way comprise an amazingly skilled and knowledgeable group of men without whose dedicated efforts much of the book's adventures would not have been possible; especially Bob Taylor, Jim Gibson and Lee Straight, who have all passed away, and Ron Grantham, who took over the organization of the Dean trips and did so much to preserve club history in the *Totems Topics*.

The completion of this book owes most to my sweetheart, and now fiancée, Cristina Martini. Recognizing the immense procrastination of which I am capable, she structured my life so that if I was writing I didn't have to tidy or reorganize the study or the utility room. Psychologically, I had no choice but to sit at the keyboard. The book is finished; those other projects remain unfinished. I am eternally grateful to Cristina. I only hope the product justifies the path of least resistance that she set me on.

And finally I owe a debt of gratitude to Ted, who repeatedly urged me to write. Poetic justice will have been done if the book serves to reveal something of significance about Ted Hughes to those who read it.